Amritsari Gobi Matar Recipe (Punjabi Style Creamy Cauliflower and Peas Curry)

Cauliflower or Gobi as it is known in Hindi, is a favourite winter time vegetable in North India. It is stuffed inside a delicious paratha or cooked along with vegetables like potatoes(aloo), peas(matar) to be served as an interesting side dish. Nowadays, Gobi is available throughout the year, thereby allowing us to consume this wonderful vegetable any time. In South India, 'Gobi' is more loved as a crunchy snack. The cauliflower (Gobi) is full of nutrients, vitamins and fibre. In this recipe, Amritsari Gobi Matar, the cauliflower and peas are cooked together in a spicy tomato cream base. This dish is healthy and is completely vegan and gluten free.

Serve Amritsari Gobi Matar along with Pudina Tawa Paratha for a delicious weekday lunch or dinner.

Prep Time	:	26 Mins
Cooks Time	:	45 Mins
Total Time	:	71 Mins
Cuisine	:	North Indian
Serving	:	4-5 Servings

Equipments Used: Preethi Blue Leaf Mixer Grinder, Hard Anodised Kadai (Wok)

Ingredients

1 Cauliflower (gobi) , cut into florets

1/2 cup Green peas (Matar)

1/8 teaspoon Turmeric powder (Haldi)

1/2 teaspoon Coriander Powder (Dhania)

1 teaspoon Red Chilli powder

1/2 teaspoon Garam masala powder

For the gravy

2 Onions

4 Tomatoes

2 Green Chillies

4 cloves Garlic

1/2 inch Ginger

For the cream

20 Whole Almonds (Badam) , soak in warm water for 15 minutes and peel the skin

15 Cashew nuts

For tempering

1 tablespoon Oil

1/2 teaspoon Cumin seeds (Jeera)

For garnish

Coriander (Dhania) Leaves , few sprigs

How to make Amritsari Gobi Matar Recipe (Punjabi Style Creamy Cauliflower and Peas Curry)

To begin making the Amritsari Gobi Matar recipe, grind the ingredients given under 'for the gravy' into a puree using a mixer grinder.

Grind the soaked and peeled almonds and cashews into a cream by adding 1/4 cup of water. You can adjust the consistency while grinding.

Heat a pan/wok with oil and temper with cumin seeds. Add the puree, turmeric powder, chilli powder, dhania powder, salt and cook over low flame for 5 to 7 minutes.

Now add the cauliflower, peas and mix well. Add 1/2 cup water (adjust) and cook them covered till the cauliflower is just done and soft but not mushy.

Add the garam masala powder and stir in the almond cashew cream and let it come to a boil.

Switch off, garnish with cilantro leaves and serve hot. Serve Amritsari Gobi Matar along with Pudina

Tawa Paratha for a delicious weekday lunch or
dinner.

Brahmin Style Vegetable Kurma Recipe

Brahmin Style Vegetable Kurma, is a coconut curry
that is filled with vegetables with no onion and no
garlic flavour in it. You can add vegetables of your
choice to make this Kurma.

Brahmin Style Vegetable Kurma Recipe is a No
Onion No Garlic curry which is made with loads of
vegetables and cooked in a freshly ground
coriander and coconut curry.

The spice powders that are added into the curry are
none as it is very simple and has all the flavors
from the ground paste. The curry is also made in a
Brahmin Style where they prefer to make curries
without the usage of onion and garlic. It can also

come under Satvik cooking which is a pure and natural way of consuming food.

Serve the Brahmin Style Vegetable Kurma Recipe along with Tawa Paratha, along with a Bhaji Vada Recipe (Lentil And Vegetable Fritters) by the side to enjoy your everyday lunch. You can also serve it with Steamed Rice and Carrot Methi Pachadi.

Prep Time	:	15 Mins
Cooks Time	:	20 Mins
Total Time	:	35 Mins
Cuisine	:	South Indian
Serving	:	4 Servings

Equipments Used: Preethi Blue Leaf Mixer Grinder, Hard Anodized Pressure Cooker

Ingredients

2 Carrots (Gajjar) , diced

100 grams Green beans (French Beans) , chopped in small pieces

2 Potatoes (Aloo) , skin peeled and diced

1 Green Chilli , slit

1 teaspoon Mustard seeds (Rai/ Kadugu)

1 inch Cinnamon Stick (Dalchini)

Salt , to taste

Oil

To Grind

1/2 cup Fresh coconut

2 tablespoons Roasted Gram Dal (Pottukadalai)

5 sprig Coriander (Dhania) Leaves

1 teaspoon Kala jeera

1 teaspoon Cumin seeds (Jeera)

1 Green Chilli

1 inch Ginger

1 teaspoon Turmeric powder (Haldi)

10 grams Tamarind

How to make Brahmin Style Vegetable Kurma Recipe

To begin making the Brahmin Style Vegetable Kurma Recipe, we will firstly wash, chop all the vegetables and keep it ready.

Then put all the ingredients for grinding including coconut, gram dal, coriander leaves, kala jeera, cumin seeds, green chilli, ginger, turmeric powder, tamarind into a mixer and grind into a smooth paste by adding little water.

Heat a pressure cooker with oil, add mustard seeds, cloves and cinnamon stick and wait till they splutter for a few seconds.

Add carrots, green beans, potatoes and saute them until they soften. Once the vegetables are half cooked you can add the ground paste.

After 2 minutes, add water, salt and pressure cook for about 1 whistle. Release the pressure naturally, open the cooker, give it a mix and serve the Vegetable Kurma hot.

Serve the Brahmin Style Vegetable Kurma Recipe along with Tawa Paratha, along with a Bhaji Vada Recipe (Lentil And Vegetable Fritters) by the side to enjoy your everyday lunch. You can also serve it with Steamed Rice and Carrot Methi Pachadi.

Subz Noor E Chashm Recipe (Nawabi Curry Recipe)

Subz Noor E Chashm Recipe (Nawabi Curry Recipe) is a rich and creamy curry filled with assorted vegetables which go well with Indian bread. The curry was originally from Awadhi cuisine, which was a feast for all the royal families. Thus the gravy consists of almonds and cashew nuts to give it a rich and luscious consistency.

The curry can be made with any different kinds of assorted vegetables that are locally grown at your place to make a delicious and comforting meal for the day.

Serve the Subz Noor E Chashm Recipe (Nawabi Curry Recipe) along with whole wheat Lachha Paratha to enjoy the Awadhi Meal.

Prep Time	:	20 Mins
Cooks Time	:	30 Mins
Total Time	:	50 Mins
Cuisine	:	Awadhi
Serving	:	4 Servings

Equipment Used: Hard Anodised Biryani Pan/ Large Cooking Pot.

Ingredients

1 Cauliflower (gobi) , cut into small florets and blanched

1/2 cup Green peas (Matar)

1 Carrot (Gajjar) , cubed and blanched

1 Bay leaves (tej patta)

3 Cloves (Laung) , 3 cloves

1/2 teaspoon Cumin seeds (Jeera)

3 cloves Garlic , chopped

1 inch Ginger , chopped

1 teaspoon Turmeric powder (Haldi)

1 teaspoon Red Chilli powder ,

2 teaspoons Garam masala powder

For the Paste

1 teaspoon Cumin seeds (Jeera)

2 Onions , chopped

2 Tomatoes , chopped

2 tablespoons Cashew nuts

2 tablespoons Whole Almonds (Badam) , blanched

1/2 cup Curd (Dahi / Yogurt)

Salt , taste

Oil , for cooking

1 sprig Coriander (Dhania) Leaves , for garnish

How to make Subz Noor E Chashm Recipe (Nawabi Curry Recipe)

We begin making the Subz Noor E Chashm Recipe (Nawabi Curry Recipe) by making the paste for the curry, heat a non-stick pan and crackle the cumin seeds. Add onions and saute till it is translucent and golden brown.

Later on add the chopped tomatoes, cook till it becomes mushy and soft. Add in the nuts and saute for 2 more minutes. Remove it from the flame and let it cool so you can blend it into a smooth paste using a blender.Once it is done, mix it with curd and combine it evenly.

Next is to make the curry, heat a flat bottomed pan and pour some oil, add in the cumin seeds, ginger and garlic. Saute till it is brown. Add all the vegetables and saute for about 10 minutes.

Once the vegetables are cooked a little,add the ground paste and coat it evenly. Add the spice powders that are listed and cook again for 4 more minutes.

You can adjust the consistency by adding some water and bringing it to a boil. Check for seasoning, according to your taste.

Serve the Subz Noor E Chashm Recipe (Nawabi Curry Recipe) along with whole wheat Lachha Paratha to enjoy the Awadhi Meal.

Hyderabadi Shahi Mixed Vegetable Curry Recipe

Rich and delicious, Hyderabadi Shahi Mixed Vegetable Curry is a mouth watering curry which can be served with Paratha and a Raita of your choice.

The Hyderabadi Shahi Mixed Vegetable Curry Recipe is a rich gravy dish that has a creamy texture, lots of vegetables, has a spicy taste and is packed with flavors. The addition of almond paste into the recipe adds great flavors and the richness to the Shahi Mixed Vegetable Curry.

Serve the Shahi Mixed Vegetable Curry along with Whole Wheat Lachha Paratha Recipe, Palak Raita and Pickle for a weeknight dinner or even as a main course for a party.

Prep Time	:	30 Mins
Cooks Time	:	40 Mins
Total Time	:	70 Mins
Cuisine	:	Hyderabadi
Serving	:	4 Servings

Equipments Used: Hard Anodized Pressure Cooker, Stainless Steel 2 Tier Steamer

Ingredients

12 Baby Potatoes , boiled peeled and cubed

1/4 cup Green peas (Matar)

2 Carrots (Gajjar) , diced

10 Green beans (French Beans) , cut into 2 inch pieces

1 Red Bell pepper (Capsicum) , diced

1 Yellow Bell Pepper (Capsicum) , diced

2 tablespoons Sultana Raisins

1/4 cup Tomato , puree

1 Onion , finely chopped

3 cloves Garlic

1 inch Ginger

1 teaspoon Red Chilli powder

1/2 teaspoon Turmeric powder (Haldi)

1 teaspoon Garam masala powder

1 teaspoon Coriander Powder (Dhania)

1/2 teaspoon Cumin powder (Jeera)

1 Bay leaves (tej patta)

3 tablespoons Cashew nuts

3 tablespoons Fresh cream

2 sprig Coriander (Dhania) Leaves , finely chopped

Salt , as per taste

Oil , for cooking

How to make Hyderabadi Shahi Mixed Vegetable Curry Recipe

To begin making the Hyderabadi Shahi Mixed Vegetable Curry Recipe, we will first prepare the vegetables for the curry.

Boil the potatoes, either in water or in the pressure cooker for about 3 whistles until just about cooked. Once cooked allow the potatoes to cool a bit, peel the skin and dice the baby potatoes. Keep this aside.

Steam the remaining vegetables in a steamer until just about cooked through. Take care to not overcook them. The steamer takes just about 5 minutes to cook the vegetables on high heat. Once cooked, keep aside.

Heat a couple of teaspoons of oil in a heavy bottomed pan, add the onions, ginger and garlic and saute until soft and lightly browned and the raw smell has gone away. Turn off the heat and let it cool. Once cooled, make a paste of the onion ginger and garlic - keep this aside.

Make the tomato puree according to the recipe on the link and keep aside.

Make a paste of the cashew nuts adding little water to make a smooth cream-like paste. Keep this cashew nut paste aside.

The next step is to begin cooking the Shahi Vegetable Curry.

In the same heavy bottomed pan we cooked the onion, add a teaspoon of oil. Add the red and yellow bell peppers and stir fry them until they are softened and well roasted.

Add the onion garlic paste, bay leaf and turmeric powder. Saute the onion mixture until the paste is cooked and comes together and leaves oil around the edges.

Next, add tomato puree along with red chili powder, bay leaf, coriander powder, cumin powder, salt and garam masala. Stir until everything is completely combined.

Give the Shahi Curry mixture a brisk boil and add in the cooked potatoes and steamed vegetables. Turn the heat to low, add a little water, cover the pan and simmer the Hyderabadi Shahi Mixed Vegetable Curry for about 5 minutes until all the vegetables get the flavors of the masala.

Finally stir in the cashew nut cream and the fresh cream into the Shahi Curry and simmer for another 3 to 4 minutes. Turn off the heat. Check the salt and spice levels and adjust to suit your taste.

Stir in the chopped coriander leaves and serve.

Serve the Shahi Mixed Vegetable Curry along with Whole Wheat Lachha Paratha Recipe, Palak Raita and Pickle for a weeknight dinner or even as a main course for a party.

Sweet Potato & Neem Leaves Vegetable Curry Recipe

Neem & Sweet potato have extreme differences in taste but have numerous health benefits. I combined them into a single healthy dish by making this simple Sweet Potato & Neem Leaves Vegetable Curry Recipe. The vegetable curry's flavor is further enhanced with roasted peanut powder. The dish is definitely sweet & bitter with bitterness slightly overriding.

Consuming neem leaves at least weekly once or twice is very good but we do not have many recipes using them. Serve Sweet Potato & Neem Leaves Vegetable Curry Recipe with a rasam rice for lunch, it tastes awesomely bittersweet!

Prep Time   :   20 Mins

Cooks Time   :   30 Mins

Total Time	:	50 Mins
Cuisine	:	Indian
Serving	:	4 Servings

Equipments Used: Hard Anodised Kadai (Wok)

Ingredients

4 Sweet Potatoes

1/2 cup Neem leaves

1/4 teaspoon Asafoetida (hing)

1/3 teaspoon Mustard seeds (Rai/ Kadugu)

1/3 teaspoon White Urad Dal (Split)

1 Dry Red Chilli

1 teaspoon Chana dal (Bengal Gram Dal)

1.5 tablespoon Oil

Salt , to taste

1 tablespoon Roasted Peanuts (Moongphali) , powdered

How to make Sweet Potato & Neem Leaves Vegetable Curry Recipe

To prepare Sweet Potato & Neem Leaves Vegetable Curry Recipe, clean the neem leaves and tear the stem out of it.

Pressure cook the sweet potato for just 1 whistle or 5 minutes whichever is earlier, on full flame. The pressure will take longer if you put in a lot of water.

Take out, peel & chop them into cubes.

Take a non-stick pan, add oil, hing, mustard, urad dhal, red chilli & bengal gram dal. Fry them well.

Add the neem leaves and let it fry for 3-4 minutes until they turn slightly crispy.

Add the chopped sweet potato and salt. Cook well until the sweet potato is fried well.

Garnish with roasted peanut powder.

Serve Sweet Potato & Neem Leaves Vegetable Curry Recipe with hot steaming rasam rice.

Karwar Style Khatkhate Recipe (Mixed Vegetable Curry With Toor Dal & Coconut)

Karwar Style Khatkhate Recipe is basically a konkani mixed vegetable curry that is cooked along with toor dal and coconut milk. Serve the comforting curry along with lashani kadhi and phulka.

Karwar Style Khatkhate Recipe (Mixed Vegetable Curry With Toor Dal & Coconut) is basically a konkani mixed vegetable curry with toor dal and coconut. This dish is common in almost all konkani houses.

A variety of mixed seasonal veggies are used to make Khatkhate. It's a no onion no garlic dish. Addition of tirphal or Sichuan pepper gives a unique flavour to this curry.

Serve Karwar Style Khatkhate Recipe (Mixed Vegetable Curry With Toor Dal & Coconut) along with Karwar Style Lasani Kadhi and Steamed Rice for a weekday meal.

Prep Time	:	10 Mins
Cooks Time	:	20 Mins
Total Time	:	30 Mins
Cuisine	:	Karnataka
Serving	:	4 Servings

Equipments Used: Hard Anodised Kadai (Wok)

Ingredients

1/2 cup Arhar dal (Split Toor Dal)

2 cups Mixed vegetables , (beans, carrot, potato, peas, drumstick, radish, taro root)

1/2 teaspoon Turmeric powder (Haldi)

2 tablespoons Jaggery , adjustable

5 Kokum (Malabar Tamarind) , soak in hot water and extract juice

Salt , to taste

For the gravy

1/2 Fresh coconut , grated

4 Dry Red Chillies

1/2 teaspoon Coriander Powder (Dhania)

8 Sichuan peppercorns

For tempering

2 teaspoons Oil

1 teaspoon Mustard seeds (Rai/ Kadugu)

1/2 teaspoon Cumin seeds (Jeera)

Curry leaves , few

How to make Karwar Style Khatkhate Recipe (Mixed Vegetable Curry With Toor Dal & Coconut)

To begin making the Karwar Style Khatkhate Recipe, wash and pressure cook toor dal with a pinch of turmeric for 2-3 whistles. Once cooked, mash it well and keep aside.

Dice the vegetables and cook them with enough water in a pressure cooker for one whistle. Turn off the flame and immediately release the pressure. They should just be cooked. make sure you don't overcook them.

Meanwhile, grind coconut, red chillies, coriander powder and turmeric powder with little water to a smooth paste. Add sichuan pepper and grind the paste again for a few more seconds.

When the vegetables are almost done, add ground coconut paste and mashed toor dal. Add salt, kokam and jaggery. Mix everything well and bring to a boil .

Finally, prepare the tempering for the curry. Heat oil in a kadhai. Add mustard seeds, cumin seeds and curry leaves. Cook for about a minute and then pour it on Khatkhate.

Serve Karwar Style Khatkhate Recipe (Mixed Vegetable Curry With Toor Dal & Coconut) along with Karwar Style Lasani Kadhi and Steamed Rice for a weekday meal.

Mustard Vegetable Curry Recipe

The Mustard Vegetable Curry is made from a delicious blend of Dijon Mustard, mixed vegetables and a subtle set of ingredients like cumin, chilli, and coconut milk. The dijon mustard and the coconut milk make a delicious and unique combination for a curry, making it perfect to be served along with a crusted bread or even steamed rice or tawa paratha for dinner.

Prep Time   :   20 Mins

Cooks Time   :   30 Mins

Total Time   :   50 Mins

Cuisine   :   Indian

Serving   :   4 Servings

Equipments Used: Hard Anodised Kadai (Wok)

Ingredients

2 teaspoons Oil

1 teaspoon Cumin seeds (Jeera)

2 cloves Garlic , grated

2 Onions , finely chopped

1 teaspoon Red Chilli powder

1/2 teaspoon Turmeric powder (Haldi)

120 ml Coconut milk

1 cup Vegetable stock

2 tablespoons Dijon Mustard

2 Carrots (Gajjar) , cut into rounds or lengthwise of 1 inch thickness

5 to 6 Green beans (French Beans) , cut into 1 inch pieces, steamed

1/4 cup Green peas (Matar) , steamed

2 Potatoes (Aloo) , boiled and diced small

Salt , to taste

How to make Mustard Vegetable Curry Recipe

To begin making the Mustard Vegetable Curry Recipe, we will first have to steam the vegetables and keep them ready. You can use a steamer or a pressure cooker to cook the vegetables.

Potatoes take a longer time to cook, so I suggest you cook them separately from the beans, carrots and peas.

To begin making the curry base; heat a teaspoon of oil in a pan on medium heat. Add in the cumin seeds, garlic and onion and saute on medium heat until the onion has turned light pink and translucent.

Once the onions are ready; add in the turmeric powder, chilli powder and stir for a few seconds. Finally add in the coconut milk, the vegetable stock and the dijon mustard.

Add in the salt and check the spice and salt levels. Adjust to suit your taste.

Finally stir in the steamed vegetables; turn the heat to low, cover the pan and simmer the curry for 3 to 4 minutes. Turn off the heat and the Mustard Vegetable Curry is ready to be served.

Serve the Mustard Vegetable Curry hot with steamed rice or tawa paratha for dinner.

Goan Vegetable Curry Recipe

Goan Vegetable Curry is a classic dish from Goa. It is a part of a day to day meal. It is filled with the goodness of vegetables and you can also add vegetables of your choice to make this curry.

Goan Vegetable Curry Recipe is a classic dish from Goa. It is a part of a day to day meal. It is made with mixed vegetables. This dish is simple and easy to make.You can add vegetables according to your taste and preference. It's creamy and coconut based and will spice up your everyday meal.

Serve Goan Vegetable Curry Recipe along with Beetroot Raita and Whole Wheat Lachha Paratha for a weekday meal.

Prep Time	:	15 Mins
Cooks Time	:	20 Mins
Total Time	:	35 Mins
Cuisine	:	Goan
Serving	:	4 Servings

Equipments Used: Hard Anodised Kadai (Wok)

Ingredients

4 cups Mixed vegetables , French beans, carrots, peas, potatoes, cauliflower, squash)

1 Onion

Salt , to taste

1/2 teaspoon Turmeric powder (Haldi)

1 Green Chilli

1 teaspoon Coconut Oil

For the masala

100 grams Fresh coconut , grated

4 Kashmiri dry red chillies

1/2 teaspoon Whole Black Peppercorns

1/2 Onion , sliced

4 cloves Garlic

1 tablespoon Coriander (Dhania) Seeds

1 teaspoon Cumin seeds (Jeera)

1 Tamarind , lemon size

How to make Goan Vegetable Curry Recipe

To begin making the Goan Vegetable Curry Recipe, clean and chop the vegetables into cubes.

Add oil in a heavy bottomed pan and add onions. Cook till the onions become translucent.

Add remaining vegetables, turmeric powder, green chillies and required amount of water. Cook on medium flame till it is done.

Meanwhile, grind all the ingredients mentioned under masala including coconut, kashmiri dry red chillies, whole black peppercorns, onion, garlic, coriander seeds, cumin seeds, tamarind to a smooth paste.

Add the masala paste and salt to the cooked vegetables. Cook on sim till the raw smell from curry goes and keep stirring in between. This will take about 5 to 7 minutes.

Switch off when the curry is cooked properly. Serve hot.

Serve Goan Vegetable Curry Recipe along with Beetroot Raita and Whole Wheat Lachha Paratha for a weekday meal.

Mixed Vegetable Poricha Kootu Recipe (Steamed Vegetable in Coconut and Lentil Curry)

Mixed Vegetable Poricha Kootu is a delicious preparation of the steamed vegetables that is cooked in a coconut and lentil curry. The Poricha Kootu is a traditional south Indian recipe that is great comfort food. Serve the Mixed Vegetable Poricha Kootu along with steamed rice and Vathal Kozhambu.

Prep Time   :   20 Mins

Cooks Time   :   45 Mins

Total Time   :   65 Mins

Cuisine   :   Tamil Nadu

Serving   :   4 Servings

Equipments Used: Hard Anodised Kadai (Wok)

Ingredients

1 Chayote , or snake gourd, peeled and cubed

100 grams Green beans (French Beans) , chopped

3 Carrots (Gajjar) , peeled and chopped

1/2 cup Green Moong Dal (Split)

1/2 teaspoon Turmeric powder (Haldi)

Ingredients to be ground to paste

1/2 cup Fresh coconut , grated

4 Dry Red Chilli

1 teaspoon Cumin seeds (Jeera)

5 Curry leaves

Salt , to taste

Ingredients for Seasoning

1 teaspoon Oil

4 Curry leaves

1 teaspoon Mustard seeds (Rai/ Kadugu)

1 teaspoon White Urad Dal (Split)

1 teaspoon Chana dal (Bengal Gram Dal) , 1
teaspoon bengal gram

How to make Mixed Vegetable Poricha Kootu Recipe (Steamed Vegetable in Coconut and Lentil Curry)

To begin making the Mixed Vegetable Poricha
Kootu Recipe; we will first cook the moong dal
lentils with about 2 cups of water in a saucepan or

a pressure cooker, along with a 1/4 teaspoon of turmeric powder.

Once cooked completely, whisk it using a fork.

Steam the chow-chow, the beans and carrots adding just a little salt, until tender and cooked.

Grind together the grated coconut, cumin seeds, curry leaves and the red chilli into a smooth paste. Use warm water for grinding, this will help the coconut blend well with the chillies.

Heat oil in a heavy bottomed pan; add the mustard seeds, bengal gram and halved white urad dal and allow them to crackle. Allow the dal to roast well until lightly browned.

Stir in the cooked lentils, the cooked vegetables and curry leaves and sauté for a few minutes. Add a little water to adjust the consistency of the Mixed Vegetable Poricha Kootu. Check the salt levels and adjust to suit your taste.

Serve the Mixed Vegetable Poricha Kootu along with steamed rice and Vathal Kozhambu.

Poricha Kuzhambu Recipe (Tamil Nadu Style Mixed Vegetables and Lentil Stew)

Poricha Kuzhambu is a traditional recipe from the Tirunelveli region of Tamil Nadu. It is a mixed vegetables and lentil stew, prepared using the mildly spiced coconut mix. It makes for a wonderful side dish with steamed rice. Since it uses mild spices, it is easy on the tummy as well.

Serve the Poricha Kuzhambu along with steamed rice, Manathakkali Kai Vathal Kuzhambu, Carrot and Beans Poriyal Recipe and potato roast for a full course Tamil Nadu style lunch menu on the weekend.

Prep Time   :   10 Mins

Cooks Time   :   20 Mins

Total Time	:	30 Mins
Cuisine	:	Tamil Nadu
Serving	:	4 Servings

Equipments Used: Hard Anodized Pressure Cooker, Tadka Pan (Seasoning Pan)

Ingredients

1/2 cup Arhar dal (Split Toor Dal) , cooked

1/2 cup Carrots (Gajjar) , finely chopped

1/2 cup Green peas (Matar)

1/2 cup Green beans (French Beans) , finely chopped

1/2 cup Cauliflower (gobi) , cut into small florets

2 tablespoons Fresh coconut , grated

1 teaspoon Cumin seeds (Jeera)

2 Dry Red Chilli

1 teaspoon Rice , soaked

1/2 teaspoon Turmeric powder (Haldi)

1 teaspoon Mustard seeds (Rai/ Kadugu)

1/2 teaspoon White Urad Dal (Split)

1 sprig Curry leaves

Salt , to taste

How to make Poricha Kuzhambu Recipe (Tamil Nadu Style Mixed Vegetables and Lentil Stew)

To begin making Poricha Kuzhambu, wash and soak the toor dal for 30 minutes and then pressure cook using a cooker for 3 whistles and keep aside.

Make a smooth paste of grated coconut, soaked raw rice, cumin seeds and red chillies using a hand blender and keep aside.

Now take a big wok, add all the vegetables, 1/2 glass of water, turmeric powder, salt and cook until the vegetables are well cooked in medium flame.

Add the cooked dal to the vegetables, water to your required consistency and bring it to a rolling boil.

Now, add the ground spice mix, season with salt and let it simmer for 10 minutes to thicken and switch off the flame.

Heat a small tadka pan on medium heat, add the mustard seeds and urad dal and let it crackle.

Add the curry leaves and let it splutter and pour this tadka over the Poricha Kuzhambu.

Serve the Poricha Kuzhambu along with steamed rice, Manathakkali Kai Vathal Kuzhambu, Carrot and Beans Poriyal Recipe and potato roast for a full course Tamil Nadu style lunch menu on the weekend.

Yeruvalli Kuzhambu Recipe | Iru Puli Kuzhambu | Tangy Coconut Curry

Give this lip smacking Yeruvalli Kuzhambu a try. It is a tangy and spicy coconut curry with vegetables making it perfect to go along with hot steamed rice and potato roast.

The Yeruvalli Kuzhambu Recipe also known as Iru Puli Kuzhambu is a very popular dish among the Tamil Brahmin and Kerala Tamil Brahmin community. This Kuzhambu recipe is made from freshly grated coconut, roasted fenugreek seeds, dried red chillies and cooked along with tamarind to make it a spicy curry.

A variety of vegetables can be used for the Yeruvalli Kuzhambu Recipe. The most popular combinations are the drumsticks, carrots and green bell peppers or cut okra or eggplants. Experiment and add vegetables to suit your palate. The recipe below uses carrots and green bell pepper. The Yeruvalli Kuzhambu can be served along with hot steamed rice and dosa.

Serve the Yeruvalli Kuzhambu / Iru Puli Kuzhambu along with hot steamed rice for lunch and or even along with dosa's.

Prep Time   :   10 Mins

Cooks Time   :   30 Mins

Total Time   :   40 Mins

Cuisine   :   South Indian

Serving   :   4 Servings

Equipments Used: Hard Anodized Pressure Cooker, Hard Anodised Kadai (Wok), Tadka Pan (Seasoning Pan)

Ingredients

1 Carrots (Gajjar) , peeled and diced

1 Green Bell Pepper (Capsicum) , diced

1 Drumstick , cut into 1 inch pieces

1 cup Tamarind Water

1 teaspoon Salt

For Coconut Masala

1 cup Fresh coconut , grated

4 Dry Red Chillies

1/2 teaspoon Methi Seeds (Fenugreek Seeds)

1-1/2 teaspoons White Urad Dal (Split)

Ingredients for the Seasoning

1 teaspoon Mustard seeds (Rai/ Kadugu)

1 sprig Curry leaves

1 teaspoon Coconut Oil

How to make Yeruvalli Kuzhambu Recipe | Iru Puli Kuzhambu | Tangy Coconut Curry

To begin making the Yeruvalli Kuzhambu/ Iru Puli Kuzhambu, the first step is to prep all the ingredients and keep them ready.

Cook the vegetables along with the tamarind water in the pressure cooker. Place the diced vegetables, the tamarind water and salt into the pressure cooker.

Place the weight on and pressure cook until you heat 2 to 3 whistles. Turn off the heat and allow the pressure to release naturally.

While the pressure is getting released, we will make the curry paste for the Yeruvalli Kuzhambu/ Iru Puli Kuzhambu.

In a small pan; add in the fenugreek seeds/ methi, urad dal and red chillies. Roast them until you notice the ingredients turning slightly brown and releasing a roasted aroma.

Add the roasted ingredients into a small blender jar, add the coconut and about 1/4 cup of warm water. Blend to make a smooth curry paste.

Heat oil in a pan; add mustard seeds and curry leaves and allow it to crackle. Once it crackles, add the cooked vegetables along with the tamarind water, the coconut curry paste and give it a stir.

Check the salt levels and adjust to suit your taste. Give the Yeruvalli Kuzhambu a brisk boil and turn off the heat. Adjust the consistency of the Kuzhambu by adding 1/4 cup of water if required.

Transfer the kuzhambu to a serving bowl and serve hot.

Serve the Yeruvalli Kuzhambu / Iru Puli Kuzhambu along with hot steamed rice for lunch and or even along with dosa's.

Karwar NKGSB Style Bharli Vangi Recipe - Brinjal Curry

Bharli Vangi is a delicious combination of brinjals and roasted masalas. Absolutely lip smacking, serve this Sabzi along with Raita and Paratha or with a Konkani Dal and Steamed Rice.

Karwar NKGSB Style Bharli Vangi Recipe - Brinjal Curry is what stuffed brinjals vegetable is called in Konkani language and in Hindi it's called Bharwa Baingan. Vangi or Brinjals are of different types like the small black ones, or the surati vangi, or white vangi or the ones I have used here i.e. Kateri Vangi. The Kateri vangi are a little big in size with a slightly purplish colour like stripes and are sweet in taste. These are generally used to make the Bharli Vangi.

Brinjals are called the King of vegetables. High on nutrients, this vegetable has many health benefits and hence must be included in one's diet. Although many people don't like brinjals, if cooked differently with a delicious masala filling, they will surely love it.

With Karwar's proximity to the sea, there is an abundance of coconuts in this area. The NKGSB cuisine of Karwar uses a lot of coconuts in their cooking. This is complemented by the use of jaggery. Bharli Vangi too is a coconut based vegetable. As potatoes go very well with this vegetable, we have used a few in this recipe as well. Instead of the regular potatoes, baby potatoes too can be stuffed and used in this vegetable.

Serve Karwar NKGSB Style Bharli Vangi Recipe - Brinjal Curry along with Vali Bhaji Ambat and Steamed Rice for a weekday meal with your family.

Prep Time	:	30 Mins
Cooks Time	:	45 Mins
Total Time	:	75 Mins
Cuisine	:	Karnataka
Serving	:	4 Servings

Equipment Used: Hard Anodized Pressure Cooker, Hard Anodised Kadai (Wok), Preethi Zodiac 750-Watt Mixer Grinder.

Ingredients

6 Brinjal (Baingan / Eggplant)

2 Potato (Aloo)

1-1/2 Onion , finely chopped

1 cup Fresh coconut , grated

1/2 teaspoon Turmeric powder (Haldi)

3/4 teaspoon Tamarind

3 cloves Garlic

1/2 inch Ginger

2 tablespoons Jaggery

1 teaspoon Gram flour (besan)

1/4 cup Coriander (Dhania) Leaves , chopped

Salt , to taste

Whole spices to be roasted

2 Cloves (Laung)

1 inch Cinnamon Stick (Dalchini)

1 Cardamom (Elaichi) Pods/Seeds

2 Whole Black Peppercorns

3 Byadagi Dried Chillies

For grinding to a paste

1 tablespoon Oil

1 Onion , thinly sliced

1 cup Fresh coconut , grated

For tempering

1 tablespoon Oil

1/2 teaspoon Mustard seeds (Rai/ Kadugu)

1/4 teaspoon Asafoetida (hing)

1 sprig Curry leaves

How to make Karwar NKGSB Style Bharli Vangi Recipe - Brinjal Curry

To begin making the Karwar NKGSB Style Bharli Vangi Recipe - Brinjal Curry, first wash the brinjals thoroughly with water.

Cut off the stem and make two semi slits in it from the top to get a + sign. This is for stuffing the masala. Immerse in sufficient water till use.

Cut the potatoes into thick wedges or large chunks and immerse in sufficient water.

Next, heat a small kadhai and add the oil. Add to it the mentioned whole spices including cloves, cardamom, cinnamon stick, whole black peppercorns, byadgi red chillies and roast a little till they splutter. Remove from heat and set aside to cool.

Heat some oil in the same pan, add sliced onions and saute till they turn soft and transparent.

Now add the coconut and roast for a while. As soon as the coconut browns a little, switch off the flame and set aside to cool.

Grind together the roasted onion coconut mixture, the roasted whole spices, ginger, garlic, tamarind and jaggery in the end using sufficient water to get a thick paste.

Mix the besan in the above mixture. It helps in thickening the gravy.

Add the turmeric powder, chopped onions and salt as well, to the above mixture. Add some chilli powder if desired.

Stuff the vaangi (baingan) with this masala and keep them aside.

Heat a pressure cooker and add the oil to it. Add the mustard seeds. When they splutter add the asafoetida and the curry leaves.

After 20 seconds, add the stuffed brinjals, potatoes and the remaining masala. Stir a little.

Add water almost upto the level of the vegetable. Close lid and cook for 3 whistles on high flame or if cooking in a saucepan, cook adding hot water as required.

When the brinjals and potatoes are well cooked and the gravy has thickened, transfer to a serving bowl and garnish with chopped coriander.

Serve Karwar NKGSB Style Bharli Vangi Recipe - Brinjal Curry along with Vali Bhaji Ambat and Steamed Rice for a weekday meal with your family.

Mulakushyam Recipe - A Mixed Vegetable Lentil Curry

A simple lentil curry with vegetables is a traditional dish from Kerala, South India. Serve it with steamed rice for a complete meal.

Mulakushyam is an easy recipe from the Palakkad Cuisine. It is a dish consisting of the combination of lentils, essentially Moong Dal cooked along with vegetables with a drizzle of coconut oil to add a Palakad touch to the recipe.

You can add any vegetable of your choice like pumpkins, gourds etc. Adding a variety of vegetables in a lentil curry ensures that you get more nutrition.

Serve the Mulakushyam along with Steamed Rice , Elai Vadam and Pisarna Manga Recipe for a quick and wholesome weeknight dinner.

Prep Time	:	18 Mins
Cooks Time	:	30 Mins
Total Time	:	48 Mins
Cuisine	:	Kerala
Serving	:	4 Servings

Equipments Used: Saucepan With Handle (Tea/Sauces)

Ingredients

1/2 cup Yellow Moong Dal (Split)

1 Chayote , peeled and diced

1 Potato (Aloo) , peeled and diced

2 Carrot (Gajjar) , peeled and diced

1/4 cup Green peas (Matar)

2 Green Chillies , slit

1 teaspoon Turmeric powder (Haldi)

Salt , to taste

Curry leaves , a sprig

1/4 teaspoon Black pepper powder

1 tablespoon Coconut Oil

How to make Mulakushyam Recipe - A Mixed Vegetable Lentil Curry

To begin making the Mulakushyam Recipe - A Mixed Vegetable Lentil Curry, first prepare the vegetables by peeling and cutting them. Wash the dal and keep aside.

We will now cook everything in a single pot, by either using a pressure cooker or using a saucepan method. If using the saucepan method, follow the same instructions as below and cook until the dal is soft and cooked through.

Place the washed dal, the chopped vegetable, slit green chillies into the pressure cooker. Add the turmeric,salt and about 2 cups of water. Place the weight on and pressure cook until you hear two whistles. After 2 whistles, turn the heat to low and simmer for a couple of minutes and turn off the heat.

Allow the pressure to release naturally. Once the pressure has released, add the curry leaves, the coconut oil, salt and pepper to taste. Stir and give the Mulakushyama brisk boil. Turn off the heat and transfer to a serving bowl.

Serve the Mulakushyam along with Steamed Rice , Elai Vadam and Pisarna Manga Recipe for a quick and wholesome weeknight dinner.

Mughlai Style Aloo Matar Gobi Gravy Recipe

Mughlai Style Aloo Matar Gobi Gravy is a delicious recipe of basic vegetables of Potato, Peas and Cauliflower cooked in a royal Mughlai Style gravy and topped with a curd and saffron mixture to give it that rich flavour.

Mughlai Style Aloo Matar Gobi Curry/Sabzi Recipe is a rich onion based gravy that will keep you wanting to eat more than just one serving. This curry is prepared with day to day vegetables such as Potato/Aloo, Matar/Peas and Gobi/Cauliflower but the gravy it is cooked in gives it that extra flavour to these humble vegetables.

This Gravy is rich as it has a brilliant finish in the addition of a decadent curd and saffron/kesar mixture. The gravy gives out a strong aroma while being cooked, making your family members come into the kitchen to have a taste while it is being cooked.

Serve this Mughlai Style Aloo Matar Gobi Curry/Sabzi Recipe along with Phulkas and Kala

Chana Salad for a simple Sunday Lunch or a Weeknight Dinner.

Prep Time	:	10 Mins
Cooks Time	:	25 Mins
Total Time	:	35 Mins
Cuisine	:	Mughlai
Serving	:	5 Servings

Equipments Used: Preethi Blue Leaf Mixer Grinder, Hard Anodised Kadai (Wok)

Ingredients

1 cup Cauliflower (gobi) , florets, cleaned

1/2 cup Green peas (Matar) , fresh

3 Potatoes (Aloo) , cut into cubes

1/2 teaspoon Saffron strands

1/4 cup Curd (Dahi / Yogurt)

2 tablespoons Butter (Salted)

1 teaspoon Cumin seeds (Jeera)

Salt , as required

For the masala

1 Onion , roughly chopped

4 Dry Red Chillies

1 teaspoon Coriander (Dhania) Seeds

1 inch Cinnamon Stick (Dalchini)

2 Cloves (Laung)

2 cloves Cardamom (Elaichi) Pods/Seeds

1/4 teaspoon Fennel seeds (Saunf)

How to make Mughlai Style Aloo Matar Gobi Gravy Recipe

To begin making the Mughlai Style Aloo Matar Gobi Curry/Sabzi Recipe, keep all your ingredients ready. Make sure to keep the cut potatoes/aloo in water to prevent it from darkening.

Add the curd into a bowl, add saffron to it and mix well until combined. Keep aside.

In a mixer-jar add roughly chopped onion, dry red chillies, coriander seeds, cinnamon, cloves, cardamom and fennel. Grind into a smooth paste adding a little water.

Heat butter on low flame in a heavy bottomed pan. Once the butter melts, add cumin seeds and let it sputter.

Now, add the ground masala and saute well. Stir and cook in medium flame until oil separates from the masala. This will take about 3 to 4 minutes.

Now add chopped vegetables - Matar, Gobi and Aloo and saute for a minute.

Pour 1/2 a cup of water and salt for cooking the vegetables. Adjust the consistency of the gravy to your choice.

Close the lid of the pan and keep it closed until the vegetables get cooked. The vegetables should not be completely soft, but should have a bit of a bite to it.

Simmer the flame and add the prepared curd saffron mixture to it. Mix and cook for 2 more minutes in a completely low flame. Turn off the flame after 2 minutes.

Serve this Mughlai Style Aloo Matar Gobi Recipe along with Phulkas and Kala Chana Salad for a simple Sunday Lunch or a Weeknight Dinner.

Vendakkai-Vazhakkai Mor Kuzhambu Recipe (Tamil Nadu Style Lady's Finger & Raw Banana Curry)

Delicious but cooling veggies in buttermilk gravy

Vendakkai-Vazhakkai Mor Kuzhambu Recipe is a Tamil Nadu Style Lady's Finger & Raw Banana Curry cooked in buttermilk. This is a popular side dish along with steamed rice. In Tamil Nadu, this Mor kuzhambu is prepared with mixed vegetables or a single vegetable, is tangy and flavourful if made with mixed vegetables.

Serve Vendakkai-Vazhakkai Mor Kuzhambu Recipe (Tamil Nadu Style Lady's Finger & Raw Banana Curry) along with steamed rice and Phulka sided with Urulaikizhangu Podi (Spicy Potato Crumble from Tamil Nadu) Recipe and Tamil Nadu Style Muttaikose Pattani Poriyal Recipe.

Prep Time	:	10 Mins
Cooks Time	:	20 Mins
Total Time	:	30 Mins
Cuisine	:	Tamil Nadu
Serving	:	4 Servings

Equipments Used: Preethi Blue Leaf Mixer Grinder, Saucepan With Handle (Tea/Sauces), Tadka Pan (Seasoning Pan)

Ingredients

2 cups Buttermilk

1 cup Bhindi (Lady Finger/Okra) , chopped

1 cup Raw Banana

1/4 teaspoon Turmeric powder (Haldi)

To be ground

1 tablespoon Broken Raw Rice

1 tablespoon Arhar dal (Split Toor Dal)

2 tablespoons Coriander (Dhania) Seeds

1/2 inch Ginger , grated

2 Green Chillies , slit

1/4 cup Fresh coconut

For tempering

1 tablespoon Mustard seeds (Rai/ Kadugu)

2 Dry Red Chillies , broken

1/2 teaspoon Asafoetida (hing)

1 sprig Curry leaves

2 teaspoons Oil

How to make Vendakkai-Vazhakkai Mor Kuzhambu Recipe (Tamil Nadu Style Lady's Finger & Raw Banana Curry)

To begin making Vendakkai-Vazhakkai Mor Kuzhambu Recipe (Tamil Nadu Style Lady's Finger & Raw Banana Curry), In a kadai, stir fry the ladies finger.

Add the raw bananas/vazhakkai once the vendakkai is half done and stir well till the sliminess of the vendakkai disappears. Make sure you stir lightly just to avoid burning and avoid them getting any mushy or breaking. Keep them aside.

Also meanwhile in a mixer grinder, grind all the ingredients mentioned under "to be ground". Once the mixture is crumbly, add water and grind further till it becomes paste-like.

In a saucepan, add a little oil. When the oil is heated, add the ground mixture, turmeric powder, cover and cook it with a little water till the rice and dal are cooked, on a medium heat. Mine took about five minutes. (you can skip adding oil here, since however the dal and rice needs to be cooked in water).

Add the buttermilk, salt and whisk it till it is properly mixed.

Add the fried vendakkai and vazhakkai (bhindi and raw bananas). Continue medium heat.

Meanwhile in a tadka pan, add oil. To this, add mustard seeds and allow to crackle. Once the mustard crackles, add asafoetida, curry leaves and dried red chillies, stir and switch off heat.

When the butter milk starts to froth up from the edges of the pan, add the tempering and turn off the flame. Do not boil after adding the butter milk.

Give Mor kuzhambu a nice mix and cover for 5 minutes before serving.

Serve Vendakkai-Vazhakkai Mor Kuzhambu Recipe (Tamil Nadu Style Lady's Finger & Raw Banana Curry) along with steamed rice and Phulka sided with Urulaikizhangu Podi (Spicy Potato

Crumble from Tamil Nadu) Recipe and Tamil Nadu Style Muttaikose Pattani Poriyal Recipe.

Broccoli And Tofu Green Curry Recipe

Fresh Broccoli florets and Tofu are cooked in a spicy green curry to make this fragrant Broccoli and Tofu green curry recipe. This is a very easy recipe and with a little advance prep work, it takes just under 20 minutes to make. You can make a stock of the green curry paste ahead of time, freeze and use as required. Broccoli and Tofu green curry recipe is served with Rice, and is perfect for a busy weeknight meal.

Prep Time   :   15 Mins

Cooks Time	:	20 Mins
Total Time	:	35 Mins
Cuisine	:	Indian
Serving	:	3 Servings

Equipments Used: Hard Anodised Kadai (Wok), Philips Food Processor

Ingredients

1 Broccoli , washed and cut into florets

250 grams Tofu , cut into cubes

2 tablespoon Oil

2 tablespoon Soy sauce , or thai fish sauce

200 ml Coconut milk

Vegetable stock , as required

Salt , to taste

Lemon wedges , to serve

Ingredients For The Curry Paste

1 Lemongrass , stalk, chopped

4-5 Thai basil leaves

1 inch Galangal , peeled and sliced (or use ginger)

2 Kaffir lime leaves , torn (or use dried leaves)

3-4 Shallots , chopped

1 sprig Coriander (Dhania) Leaves , washed and chopped

3 Garlic , minced

How to make Broccoli And Tofu Green Curry Recipe

To begin making the Broccoli and Tofu green curry recipe, first, blend the ingredients mentioned under "Curry Paste" to a fine paste, using a mortar and pestle or food processor.

Heat oil in a Kadai and add the curry paste. Sauté for 1-2 minutes till you get a nice aroma.

Add the broccoli florets, mix and stir fry for 1-2 minutes.

Add the Tofu and stir for another 1-2 minutes.

Add 1/2 - 1 cup of the vegetable stock, soy sauce, and coconut milk.

Stir and cook for 7-8 minutes till it thickens a little.

Adjust the consistency of the Broccoli and Tofu green curry as desired.

Serve the green curry recipe hot with cooked Rice and lemon wedges on the side.

Baingan Musallam Recipe (Mughlai Style Eggplant Simmered In Rich Tomato Curry)

The Baingan Musallam Recipe, is a delicious brinjals/eggplant that is simmered and cooked in a spicy and tangy tomato gravy. The addition of cream and along with the spices make it a rich and delicious Mughali dish. You can either use small brinjal and deep fry them, or like we have done, cut them into long wedges and pan roast them, making it a healthier alternative.

Serve the Baingan Musallam Recipe along with Vegetable Yakhni Pulao Recipe and Burani Raita for a delicious dinner for parties.

Prep Time   :   20 Mins

Cooks Time	:	30 Mins
Total Time	:	50 Mins
Cuisine	:	Hyderabadi
Serving	:	4 Servings

Equipments Used: Hard Anodised Kadai (Wok)

Ingredients

1 Brinjal (Baingan / Eggplant) , cut into wedges

1 cup Homemade tomato puree

1/2 teaspoon Turmeric powder (Haldi)

1 teaspoon Coriander Powder (Dhania)

1/2 teaspoon Garam masala powder

1 Bay leaf (tej patta) , torn into half

1 teaspoon Red Chilli powder

1 tablespoon Fresh cream

1 tablespoon Sultana Raisins

Coriander (Dhania) Leaves , a small bunch finely chopped

Salt , to taste

Oil , for cooking

To Make Into Paste

1 Onion , roughly chopped

3 cloves Garlic

1 inch Ginger

How to make Baingan Musallam Recipe (Mughlai Style Eggplant Simmered In Rich Tomato Curry)

To begin making the Baingan Musallam Recipe, first prep all the ingredients required. Make the tomato puree and keep aside.

Make the ginger, onion, garlic paste and keep aside.

Heat a tablespoon of oil in a Kadai/Heavy Bottomed Pan. Add the eggplant wedges, sprinkle some salt and cook the baingan in the Pan until done. Cover the pan, so that the steam that gets created will help cook the baingan faster.

Once the baingan is cooked, remove from the pan and keep aside.

In the same Pan, add the onion garlic paste and saute on medium heat until the raw smell goes away. Add all the spices, the tomato puree and cook the tomato puree along with the spices for a couple of minutes until it comes to a brisk boil.

Stir in the raisins, the roasted baingan, the cream and simmer for about 5 minutes until the masalas get well incorporated into the baingan.

Once done, check the salt and spices and adjust the taste accordingly. Stir in the chopped coriander leaves and serve.

Serve the Baingan Musallam Recipe along with Vegetable Yakhni Pulao Recipe and Burani Raita for a delicious dinner for parties.

Kollu Vada Kurma Recipe (Horse Gram Fritters Spicy & Tangy Curry)

The Kollu Vada Kurma Recipe is a fingerlicking curry to relish either with rice or with rotis, that is made from horse gram dal. The horse gram dal fritters are added in this coconut based masala gravy, making it a healthy addition to a traditional korma recipe.

Serve the Kollu Vadai Kurma along with steamed rice, topped with ghee or even along with Dosa, Idli and Upmas for breakfast.

Prep Time   :   10 Mins

Cooks Time   :   45 Mins

Total Time : 55 Mins

Cuisine : South Indian

Serving : 4 Servings

Equipments Used: Preethi Blue Leaf Mixer
Grinder, Hard Anodized Pressure Cooker, Glass
Mixing Bowl

Ingredients

For Kollu Vadai (Horse Gram Fritters)

2 cups Horse Gram Dal (Kollu/ Kulith)

1 Onion , finely chopped

2 Green Chillies , finely chopped

1 inch Ginger , finely chopped

1 sprig Curry leaves , finely chopped

1 teaspoon Fennel seeds (Saunf) , coarsely
pounded

Salt , to taste

Oil , as required

Ingredients for Kurma (Curry)

2 Onions , finely chopped

2 Tomatoes , finely chopped

1 inch Ginger , grated

3 cloves Garlic

1 teaspoon Coriander Powder (Dhania)

1/2 teaspoon Red Chilli powder

1/2 teaspoon Turmeric powder (Haldi)

2 Cloves (Laung)

1 inch Cinnamon Stick (Dalchini)

2 Cardamom (Elaichi) Pods/Seeds

1 teaspoon Fennel seeds (Saunf)

3 sprig Mint Leaves (Pudina) , roughly chopped

2 Bay leaves (tej patta)

Oil , as required

To grind into a masala

2 tablespoon Poppy seeds , soaked in hot water

1/4 cup Fresh coconut , grated

5 Cashew nuts

How to make Kollu Vada Kurma Recipe (Horse Gram Fritters Spicy & Tangy Curry)

Method for Kollu Vada (Horse gram Fritters)

To begin making the Kollu Vada Kurma Recipe, soak the horse gram for at least two hours in warm water or overnight. Once soaked, drain the water.

Place the soaked horse gram (kollu) along with the green chilies ginger and curry leaves into a mixer grinder. Make a coarse batter.

Place the batter in a mixing bowl, add the onions, fennel seeds, salt and mix well. Check the salt and spices and adjust to suit your taste.

Prepare the Kuzhi Paniyaram Pan and place it on medium heat. Add a teaspoon of oil into each one of its cavities. Soon the kollu vadai batter into each cavity and fry until golden brown on all sides. Proceed to make the Kollu Vadai the same way and keep aside.

Method for the Korma (Curry)

In a mixer grinder, grind poppy seeds, grated coconut and cashew nuts to fine paste and keep aside. You can add a little warm water while grinding it to a paste, to get a cook consistency.

Roast the spices in a skillet till it releases a good aroma - cloves, cinnamon sticks,cardamom seeds and fennel seeds and make a fine powder of them.

Heat oil in a pressure cooker, add the onions, ginger and garlic and saute until the onions get cooked and lightly brown. Add the tomatoes, green chilies and cook until the tomatoes are softened.

Once the tomatoes are cooked, add the coriander powder, red chilly powder, spice powder and salt. Cover the pressure cooker and cook until you hear 2 whistles and turn off the heat.

Once the pressure has released, open the cooker and add the ground masala paste, add 1 cup of water and the fried kollu vadai and cook for a few minutes until you get a good korma like consistency and all the spices are absorbed into the vada.

Turn off the stove and finally stir in the chopped mint leaves and serve.

Serve the Kollu Vadai Kurma along with steamed rice, topped with ghee or even along with Dosa, Idli and Upmas for breakfast.

Matar Chi Usal Recipe - Green Peas In A Onion Tomato Gravy

Matar Chi Usal is a Maharashtrian style matar/ peas gravy that is prepared with the most basic of ingredients that can be found in any Indian Kitchen. Serve along with Rotis and Salad for simple weeknight dinner

Matar Chi Usal as said in Marathi language, means Green Peas Vegetable Curry. Green Peas, one of my most favourite vegetables, were previously available only during the winters. I remember my mom making all the different varieties of green peas dishes during that period. Matar usal, Maatar patal bhaji, Matar pattice, etc.

Matar Chi Usal Recipe is a delicious gravy recipe which is easy to make and thus you can make it for your everyday lunch or dinner.

Did you know: Green Peas are the immature seeds of dried peas often called field peas. Green peas are really powerhouses of nutrition that are a boon for our health. These peas are low in calories as compared to beans, another legume. Being high in nutrition, these sweet green peas have a large number of health benefits! Green peas being a very delicious and healthy vegetable, makes for great dishes too!

Serve Matar Chi Usal Recipe, along with Rotis/Pav and Carrot Cucumber Tomato Salad with Lemon and Coriander for a delectable weeknight dinner.

Prep Time   :   35 Mins

Cooks Time   :   40 Mins

Total Time   :   75 Mins

Cuisine   :   Maharashtrian

Serving   :   5 Servings

Equipments Used: Hard Anodised Kadai (Wok)

Ingredients

2 cups Green peas (Matar) , fresh preferably

2 Potatoes (Aloo)

2 Onions

1 Tomato

4 cloves Garlic

1/2 inch Ginger

2 tablespoons Oil

1 teaspoon Mustard seeds (Rai/ Kadugu)

1/4 teaspoon Asafoetida (hing)

1 sprig Curry leaves

1/4 teaspoon Turmeric powder (Haldi)

1 teaspoon Red Chilli powder , preferably byadgi chilli powder

1 teaspoon Kashmiri Red Chilli Powder

2 teaspoons Garam masala powder

1/4 cup Coriander (Dhania) Leaves

Salt , to taste

How to make Matar Chi Usal Recipe - Green Peas In A Onion Tomato Gravy

To begin making the Matar Chi Usal Recipe Recipe, keep all the ingredients ready.

In a heavy bottomed pan, heat oil on medium flame. Once it's hot, add mustard seeds. As soon as they splutter, add the asafoetida.

Next, add the onions and saute. When the onions turn translucent, add the ginger garlic paste and mix well. Cook for 3-4 minutes.

When the onions are well cooked, add the turmeric powder, red chilli powder and saute. Cook For about a minute or two.

Now, add the drained cubed potatoes and mix. Add 1 cup of water to cover the potatoes and bring to a boil.

Cover and cook until the potatoes are half cooked. This will take about 10-12 minutes. Once the potatoes are half cooked, add green peas, chopped tomatoes and mix well.

Adjust the consistency of the gravy and cover and let the Matar Chi Usal cook.

Finally, add the garam masala and salt to taste.

Cover and cook until you get the desired thickness of the Matar Chi Usal gravy. Turn off the heat and garnish with chopped coriander leaves. Matar Chi Usal is ready to be served.

Serve Matar Chi Usal Recipe, along with Rotis and Carrot Cucumber Tomato Salad with Lemon and Coriander for a delectable weeknight dinner.

Mullangi Mor Pachadi Recipe (Radish in spicy tempered Yogurt Gravy Recipe)

A diabetic friendly Yogurt gravy mixed with spicy tempered radish.

Mullangi Mor Pachadi Recipe (Radish in spicy tempered Curd Gravy Recipe) is a wonderful way to add radish in curd to make a spicy curry. The sourness from the curd complements well with the flavor of the radish. Radish is a diabetic friendly vegetable as it is considered as one of the nutritional root vegetables. It is rich in Vitamin C and minerals such as iron and magnesium.

Serve the Mullangi Mor Pachadi Recipe (Radish in spicy tempered Curd Gravy Recipe) with just hot steam rice or can be had with any stuffed paratha.

Prep Time	:	5 Mins
Cooks Time	:	10 Mins
Total Time	:	15 Mins
Cuisine	:	Tamil Nadu
Serving	:	4 Servings

Equipments Used: Small Skillet (Shallow Fry Pan/ Omelette Pan)

Ingredients

1 cup Mooli/ Mullangi (Radish) , grated

1 cup Hung Curd (Greek Yogurt)

Salt , to taste

For the tempering

1 tablespoon Oil

2 Green Chillies , slit

1 teaspoon Mustard seeds (Rai/ Kadugu)

1 teaspoon White Urad Dal (Split)

1 sprig Curry leaves

1 teaspoon Asafoetida (hing)

How to make Mullangi Mor Pachadi Recipe (Radish in spicy tempered Yogurt Gravy Recipe)

We begin making the Mullangi Mor Pachadi Recipe (Radish in spicy tempered Yogurt Curry Recipe) by heating the kadai with oil, splutter mustard seeds and urad dal along with curry leaves and hing.

Add in the green chilies and grated radish. Saute till the radish is cooked and do not roast them or brown them. You can add little water and cover it with a lid and let it cook.Once done leave it to cool down.

In a bowl, whisk in the curd with salt and little water according to your consistency, add in the sauteed radish and mix well and serve.

Serve the Mullangi Mor Pachadi Recipe (Radish in spicy tempered Curd Gravy Recipe) with just hot steam rice or can be had with any stuffed paratha.

Kerala Style Pulissery Recipe (Mor Kuzhambu)

Kerala Style Pulissery Recipe (Mor Kuzhambu) is a sweet and sour yogurt based vegetable gravy from the Kerala Cuisine. At home we call it Mor Kozhambu and use ash gourd or pineapple to make this dish. During the mango season, we also use ripe mangoes. This combination of ground coconut along with yogurt simmered in pineapple, mango or ash gourd is absolutely delectable. Serve Kerala Style Pulissery Recipe (Mor Kuzhambu) with steamed rice and rotis.

Prep Time   :   20 Mins

Cooks Time	:	30 Mins
Total Time	:	50 Mins
Cuisine	:	Kerala
Serving	:	5 Servings

Equipments Used: Hard Anodised Kadai (Wok)

Ingredients

1 cup Pineapple , chunks / mango / ash gourd

1/2 teaspoon Turmeric powder (Haldi)

Salt , to taste

1 cup Curd (Dahi / Yogurt) , whisked well

Ingredients for coconut paste

1/2 cup Fresh coconut

1/2 teaspoon Cumin seeds (Jeera)

1 teaspoon Whole Black Peppercorns

1/2 teaspoon Methi Seeds (Fenugreek Seeds)

1 Curry leaves , few

Ingredients for Seasoning

1 teaspoon Oil

1/2 teaspoon Mustard seeds (Rai/ Kadugu)

5 Curry leaves , roughly torn

5 Curry leaves , roughly torn

How to make Kerala Style Pulissery Recipe (Mor Kuzhambu)

To begin making the Mor Kuzhambu recipe, we will first cook the vegetables and keep them ready. Cook the pineapple (or ash gourd or mangoes) along with salt and turmeric powder in a little bit of water on medium heat till the vegetables turn soft. I used a pressure cooker to cook the vegetables. But you can use a saucepan to cook the vegetables too. Make sure you cover the pan, so the steam that is created will help cook the vegetables faster. Keep this aside.

Next step is to make the coconut paste; for this, grind the coconut, cumin, curry leaves, fenugreek and black pepper to a fine paste adding very little water. Keep this aside.

In a heavy bottomed saucepan; add in the cooked pineapple or other vegetable you used, the coconut paste, whisked yogurt and any additional salt to taste.

Turn the heat to high and give the mixture a brisk boil. Once it comes to a brisk boil, turn off the heat as the mor kuzhambu is now ready for seasoning.

For the seasoning; heat a teaspoon of oil on medium heat; add in the mustard seeds, fenugreek seeds and curry leaves. Allow them to crackle. Add this seasoning to the above pulissery (mor kuzhambu).

Transfer the Mor Kuzhambu (Pulissery) to a serving dish and serve it along with hot rice and Beetroot Poriyal.

Note:

 You can also add local ingredients like Green Bell Peppers, Chayote Squash (Chow Chow), Carrots or Drumsticks as vegetables into the Mor Kuzhambu

Moolangi Tovve Recipe - Radish Curry

Moolangi Tovve Recipe is a mild radish curry made with a combination of mooli and yellow moong dal. Serve with hot steamed rice and a dollop of ghee for a comforting lunch.

Moolangi Tovve is a simple dal which is made with the combination of lentils and vegetables. Tovve is a Kannada term which means a simple, basic and humble dal, something that is not heavy and is light on the tummy.

Tovve is perfect for winter or rainy days and is best served with steamed rice, ghee and lemon juice squeezed on it. Tovve can be prepared with other vegetables of your choice or a combination of vegetables as well.

Serve Moolangi Tovve Recipe - Radish Curry with Steamed Rice Recipe and Elai Vadam for a comforting lunch.

Prep Time	:	10 Mins
Cooks Time	:	30 Mins
Total Time	:	40 Mins
Cuisine	:	South Indian
Serving	:	4 Servings

Equipments Used: Hard Anodized Pressure Cooker, Hard Anodised Kadai (Wok)

Ingredients

3 Mooli/ Mullangi (Radish) , peeled and sliced (5mm thick)

1/2 cup Yellow Moong Dal (Split)

1 teaspoon Turmeric powder (Haldi)

2 Green Chillies , finely chopped

1 teaspoon Ginger , grated

2 tablespoon Fresh coconut , freshly grated

For tempering

1 tablespoon Ghee

1 teaspoon Mustard seeds (Rai/ Kadugu)

2 Dry Red Chillies

1 pinch Asafoetida (hing)

For garnishing

Coriander (Dhania) Leaves , Few sprigs, finely chopped

2 Lemon wedges

How to make Mullangi Tovve Recipe - Radish Curry

To begin making Moolangi Tovve Recipe -
Radish Curry, wash the moong dal a couple of times with water and add it to the pressure cooker along with radish, turmeric powder, green chillies and 1.5 cups of water.

Pressure cook for 3 whistles. After three whistles turn off the heat and let the pressure release naturally. Once done, open the lid and keep aside.

Heat oil in a pan, add asafoetida, mustard and wait for the mustard to pop and then add red chillies and ginger and ler the red chillies crisp up.

Now add the cooked dal mixture in the pan with salt to taste and 1.5 cups of water. Brisk boil till the dal gets slightly thick.

Once it is done, add the chopped coriander and grated coconut in the Moolangi Tovve and give it a stir. Turn off the heat and transfer the Mullangi Tovve to a serving bowl and serve.

Serve Moolangi Tovve Recipe - Radish Curry with Steamed Rice Recipe and Elai Vadam for a comforting lunch.

Sweet Potato, Broccoli And Tofu Curry Recipe

Sweet Potato, Broccoli And Tofu Curry is a creamy curry filled with vegetables like sweet potato and broccoli and also tofu which can be served along with rice for a one dish meal.

Sweet Potato, Broccoli and Tofu Curry Recipe is a delicious creamy curry made with tomatoes and onions. The richness of the curry is because of the cashew nuts that are being used. The curry masala is made separate and then ground to a smooth paste and tossed in with the fresh vegetables.

The work to create this dish is very simple and all you need to do is some chopping of the vegetables. It can be your one dish meal by pairing it with some hot steamed rice or phulka and it will fill you up.

Serve the Sweet Potato, Broccoli and Tofu Curry Recipe along with Steamed Rice, Jeera Rice or Peas Pulao to enjoy everyday lunch.

Prep Time	:	10 Mins
Cooks Time	:	30 Mins
Total Time	:	40 Mins
Cuisine	:	Indian
Serving	:	4 Servings

Equipments Used: Preethi Blue Leaf Mixer Grinder, Hard Anodised Kadai (Wok)

Ingredients

1 cup Broccoli , cut into small florets

1 Sweet Potato , skin removed and cut into cubes

150 grams Tofu , cut into small cubes

1 teaspoon Kala jeera

Salt , to taste

For the gravy

1 Onion , chopped

2 Tomatoes , chopped

1 inch Ginger , chopped

4 cloves Garlic

1 Green Chilli

1 tablespoon Cashew nuts

1 teaspoon Cumin powder (Jeera)

1 teaspoon Turmeric powder (Haldi)

1 teaspoon Red Chilli powder

2 teaspoons Garam masala powder

How to make Sweet Potato, Broccoli And Tofu Curry Recipe

To begin making the Sweet Potato, Broccoli and Tofu Curry Recipe, we will first heat a sauce pan with oil, add onions, ginger and garlic and saute until it softens.

Add your spice powders including jeera powder, turmeric powder, red chilli powder and garam masala powder. Give it a mix. Add tomatoes and green chillies and little salt.

Mash it until the tomatoes get cooked and the raw smell goes away. You can add the cashew nuts now and give it a saute for 2 more minutes.

Cool it down and blend it in a mixer with water to a smooth paste.

Heat a sauce pan or kadai, add oil and once hot add cumin seeds and allow it to sparkle.

Add the sweet potato and allow it to cook and become slightly soft, later add broccoli and tofu and give it a toss for about 10 more minutes.

Add in the masala paste and mix well. Add water and salt and adjust your consistency. Leave it to simmer for 10 minutes and serve hot.

Serve the Sweet Potato, Broccoli and Tofu Curry Recipe along with Steamed Rice, Jeera Rice or Peas Pulao to enjoy everyday lunch.

Spiced Watermelon Curry Recipe With Carrots & Peppers

An easy , quick and delicious curry recipe which marries the sweet flavours of watermelon with the spicy masalas and carrots and capsicum beautifully. This curry is sure to be a hit with everyone.

The Spiced Watermelon Curry Recipe is one of those dishes that you must try when watermelons are in season. This watermelon curry is subtly spiced with ajwain and chillies, along with the addition of roasted vegetables, that bring out refreshing flavors and taste.

It is a great summer curry recipe. Carrots and capsicum along with watermelon make this recipe high in fiber and nutrition.

Serve the Spiced Watermelon Curry Recipe with Carrots & Peppers along with steamed Jasmine Rice and Carrot Cucumber Tomato Salad with Lemon and Coriander Recipe for a summery weeknight dinner.

Prep Time   :   15 Mins

Cooks Time   :   30 Mins

Total Time   :   45 Mins

Cuisine   :   Indian

Serving   :   4 Servings

Equipments Used: Hard Anodised Kadai (Wok)

Ingredients

2 cups Watermelon , cut into cubes (without skin)

1 Carrot (Gajjar) , diced

1 Green Bell Pepper (Capsicum) , diced

1 cup Homemade tomato puree

1-1/2 teaspoons Ajwain (Carom seeds)

1 teaspoon Turmeric powder (Haldi)

1 teaspoon Cumin powder (Jeera)

1/2 teaspoon Red Chilli powder

2 Dry Red Chillies

4 sprig Coriander (Dhania) Leaves , finely chopped

Salt , to taste

How to make Spiced Watermelon Curry Recipe With Carrots & Peppers

To begin making the Spiced Watermelon Curry Recipe with Carrots & Peppers Recipe, we will first make sure we have the watermelon, carrots and peppers diced and kept ready. Make sure to remove the seeds of the watermelon.

Make the homemade tomato puree and keep aside. Get all the ingredients ready and keep it by the side.

The next step is to cook the carrots and pepper.

Heat a tablespoon of oil in a heavy bottomed pan or wok. Add the ajwain seeds, carrots and bell peppers. Sprinkle some salt and stir fry until the carrots and peppers are cooked through. You can cover the pan so the vegetables get cooked faster.

Once the vegetables are cooked, add the turmeric powder, chilli powder, cumin powder and give it a stir for a few seconds. Add the tomato puree, watermelon, salt and a cup of water. Cover the pan and allow the watermelon curry to simmer for about 10 minute until you can smell flavors of the curry coming through.

After 10 minutes, check the salt and spice levels and adjust to suit your taste. Turn off the heat and transfer the watermelon curry to a serving bowl. Stir in the coriander leaves.

Serve the Spiced Watermelon Curry Recipe with Carrots & Peppers along with steamed Jasmine Rice and Carrot Cucumber Tomato Salad with Lemon and Coriander Recipe for a summery weeknight dinner.

Manathakkali Keerai Molagootal Recipe - Kootu Green And Lentil Curry In Coconut

Manathakkali Keerai Molagootal Recipe is a traditional recipe from Palakkad Kerala made using Manathakkali leaves, toor dal and a coconut masala paste. Serve with hot steamed rice for a comforting meal.

Manathakkali Keerai Molagootal (Kootu) recipe is a traditional south Indian recipe made with greens like spinach, beetroot leaves, amaranth leaves or a special greens known as Manathakkali Keerai. The Kootu is a dish in south India, that is made with the combination of lentils and coconut, mixed with green vegetables.

Simple to make, this dish is tasty and nutritious. You can pack it for your office lunch box as well along with phulkas or rice.

Serve Manathakkali Keerai Molagootal Recipe along with Steamed Rice, Kerala Olan Recipe with Pumpkin and Black Eyed Beansand Elai Vadam.

Did you know: Spinach is one of the many green leafy vegetables that have been recommended by nutritionists over the years to avoid the risk of developing diabetes.

Most pulses have a low glycemic index. It helps keep blood sugar in control. Eat frequent meals every three to four hours to prevent fluctuations in blood sugar.

Spinach is one the many green leafy vegetables that have been recommended by nutritionists over the years to avoid the risk of developing diabetes.

Prep Time	:	20 Mins
Cooks Time	:	30 Mins
Total Time	:	50 Mins
Cuisine	:	South Indian
Serving	:	4-5 Servings

Equipments Used: Hard Anodized Pressure Cooker, Saucepan With Handle (Tea/Sauces)

Ingredients

250 grams Manathakkali Keerai , washed and chopped (or any other greens like spinach, beet leaves,amaranth)

1 cup Arhar dal (Split Toor Dal)

Salt , to taste

Ingredients to be ground

1/2 cup Fresh coconut , grated

1 teaspoon White Urad Dal (Split)

3 Dry Red Chillies

1 teaspoon Cumin seeds (Jeera)

Ingredients for seasoning

1 teaspoon Coconut Oil

5 Curry leaves

1 teaspoon Mustard seeds (Rai/ Kadugu)

1 teaspoon White Urad Dal (Split)

How to make Manathakkali Keerai Molagootal Recipe - Kootu Green And Lentil Curry In Coconut

To begin making the Manathakkali Keerai Molagootal Recipe, we will first steam the greens. I like to cook it in the pressure cooker adding just a little water (about 3 tablespoons) for just one whistle. After the first whistle, release the pressure immediately. This way the greens retain the rich green colour. Once the keerai is cooked, keep it aside while we prepare the remaining ingredients.

Next, cook the lentils in a pressure cooker or sauce pan with about 2-1/2 cups of water, along with 1/4 teaspoon of turmeric powder. Once cooked completely, mash the lentils well with a wooden masher, or whisk it using a hand blender and set it aside. Watch how to cook lentils in a pressure cooker

In your next step we will dry roast the ingredients to be ground. In a small pan; add in the cumin seeds, halved urad dal and the dry red chillies. Dry roast them on medium heat until they are browned. Once roasted, turn off the heat. Grind this roasted mixture along with the coconut and turmeric powder to make a coarse paste, adding a little water at a time.

In our next step to make the Keerai Molagootal Recipe, in a large saucepan, combine the cooked spinach, lentils and the ground coconut mixture. Adjust the salt levels according to taste. Place the saucepan on medium heat and allow the mixture to come to a bowl.

While the mixture is boiling; we will prepare the seasoning for the Manathakkali Keerai Molagootal Recipe. Heat a teaspoon of coconut oil or regular cooking oil in a pan; add in the mustard seeds, split urad dal and allow them to crackle. Saute until the urad dal turns golden brown in colour. Finally stir in the curry leaves to the seasoning and turn off the heat.

Pour this seasoning mixture over the Manathakkali Keerai Molagootal and give it a stir. Turn off the heat. Transfer the Molagootal into a serving dish.

Serve Manathakkali Keerai Molagootal Recipe along with Steamed Rice, Kerala Olan Recipe with Pumpkin and Black Eyed Beansand Elai Vadam.

Mambhazam Pulissery Recipe

Mambazha Pulissery Recipe is a traditional Kerala Recipe of ripe mangoes cooked in a yogurt based curry with a flavoursome South Indian tadka. This pulissery goes perfectly with rice and a thoran by the side for a wholesome Kerala lunch meal.

Mambazha Pulissery Recipe is a traditional Kerala cuisine and is prepared by cooking vegetables in a curd and yogurt. It has subtle flavors of spiciness and tanginess.

This authentic recipe is commonly prepared in all households for Onam and served as an accompaniment for rice. Fresh ripe juicy mangoes are cooked with spice powders in a coconut based yogurt gravy.

The recipe calls for very few ingredients and is a perfect dish for summer where mangoes are in season. The curry can be prepared with cucumber, pineapple or with any vegetables.

Serve your Mambazha Pulissery with Steamed Rice, Cabbage And Carrot Thoran Recipe, and Elai Vadam Recipe (A Traditional South Indian Rice Papad) for a complete South Indian meal.

You might also like other mango recipes, try them at home and serve it to your family members.

Prep Time   :   15 Mins

Cooks Time   :   30 Mins

Total Time   :   45 Mins

Cuisine   :   Kerala

Serving   :   4 Servings

Equipments Used: Hard Anodised Kadai (Wok)

Ingredients

2 Mango (Ripe) , cut into medium sized cubes

1 tablespoon Coconut Oil

1/2 teaspoon Turmeric powder (Haldi)

Salt , to taste

To grind

1/2 cup Fresh coconut , grated

1 cup Curd (Dahi / Yogurt) , thick and sour

1/2 teaspoon Cumin seeds (Jeera)

3 Green Chillies

For seasoning

1 teaspoon Coconut Oil

1/4 teaspoon Mustard seeds (Rai/ Kadugu)

1/4 teaspoon White Urad Dal (Split)

2 sprig Curry leaves

1/2 teaspoon Methi Powder (Fenugreek Powder)

2 sprig Curry leaves

2 Dry Red Chillies

How to make Mambazha Pulissery Recipe

To begin with Mambazha Pulissery, in a kadai, add coconut oil, turmeric powder, salt, mangoes and a cup of water. Cook them over medium flame until the mango pieces become soft.

Stir them often to avoid sticking at the bottom of the pan. The gravy becomes thickened once cooled down. Hence, adjust water level as per your required consistency.

Once mango pieces are cooked, gently mash them with the back of the ladle.

In a mixer, combine coconut, yogurt, cumin seeds, curry leaves add all of them and ground them to fine smooth paste

Add the grounded paste to the mango gravy and cook over medium flame until the raw smell of the paste leaves, about 8-10 minutes.

Switch off the flame and keep the gravy aside.

In a small pan, add coconut oil and add mustard seeds, urad dal, curry leaves and wait till the mustard seeds splutter.

Add seasoning to the Pulissery. Allow the gravy to settle down for about 20 minutes

Season the gravy with the roasted fenugreek powder at the time of serving

Serve your Mambazha Pulissery with Steamed Rice, Cabbage And Carrot Thoran Recipe, and Elai Vadam Recipe (A Traditional South Indian Rice Papad) for a complete South Indian meal.

Hariyali Gobi Recipe - Palak Cauliflower Curry Recipe

You must try the Hariyali Gobi , a simple and yet delicious gravy where the spiced palak curry is tossed in with pan roasted cauliflower. This dish is packed with nutrition and can be served as a main course for a quick weeknight dinner.

You must try the Hariyali Gobi , a simple and yet delicious gravy where the spiced palak curry is tossed in with pan roasted cauliflower. This dish is packed with nutrition and can be served as a main course for a quick weeknight dinner.

The Hariyali Palak gravy is similar to that of Palak paneer gravy, we have just added a little twist to the classic recipes and tried to incorporate a vegetable. Palak is a common leafy vegetable that is available in the Indian market and it is used in most of the Indian curries. It is rich in iron and is good for Diabetes.

Serve the Hariyali Gobi Recipe along with Phulka, Kadhi pakora and Spicy Paneer Pulao for a weeknight dinner.

Prep Time	:	20 Mins
Cooks Time	:	25 Mins
Total Time	:	45 Mins
Cuisine	:	North Indian
Serving	:	4 Servings

Equipments Used: Hard Anodized Pressure Cooker

Ingredients

For the Gobi

2 cups Cauliflower (gobi) , cut into big florets

1/2 teaspoon Turmeric powder (Haldi)

1 teaspoon Garam masala powder

Salt , to taste

For the Hariyali Masala

500 grams Spinach , washed and chopped

1 Tomato , chopped or pureed

2 cloves Garlic , grated

2 inch Ginger , grated

2 Green Chillies , slit

1/2 teaspoon Cumin seeds (Jeera)

1 inch Cinnamon Powder (Dalchini)

1 teaspoon Cumin powder (Jeera)

1/4 teaspoon Turmeric powder (Haldi)

1 teaspoon Garam masala powder

2 tablespoons Fresh cream

1 tablespoon Butter (Salted)

Salt , to taste

How to make Hariyali Gobi Recipe - Palak Cauliflower Curry Recipe

To begin making the Hariyali Gobi Recipe we will first pressure cook the Hariyali masala.

Heat butter into the pressure cooker over medium heat; add the cumin seeds, garlic and saute for a few seconds.

Add the cinnamon, green chillies, palak, tomatoes, cumin powder, garam masala powder, turmeric powder and cumin powder. Saute for a few seconds, add 1 tablespoon water, cover the pressure cooker and cook for one whistle and turn off the heat.

Release the pressure immediately by running it under cold water. This will help preserve the fresh green color of the palak.

Once cooked allow the palak to cool completely and then pulse it in your blender, with almost no water into a smooth puree.

Heat oil in a kadai; add chopped cauliflower and sauté with little turmeric powder, salt.

After a few seconds, sprinkle some water and cover it and cook for about 5 minutes. Once the gobi is cooked, toss in the garam masala and stir fry for a few minutes and turn off the heat.

The gobi should be firm and yet cooked.

Once done, stir in the cream into the palak curry and transfer to a serving bowl. Place the roasted gobi into the palak curry and serve the Hariyali Gobi hot.

Serve the Hariyali Gobi Recipe along with Phulka, Kadhi Pakora and Spicy Paneer Pulao for a weeknight dinner.

Sweet & Spicy Stuffed Paneer In Kofta Curry Recipe

Here is a delicious way to prepare paneer, that you can serve along with some hot phulkas smeared with ghee!

Stuffed Paneer In Kofta Curry Recipe is a unique way of preparing and presenting your paneer dish. In this recipe, paneer is stuffed with dry fruits and spices which are placed in rich and creamy gravy.

Serve your Stuffed Paneer Baskets with Punjabi Dal Tadka, Mixed Vegetable Pulao (Pilaf), Butter Garlic Naan, Kela Anar Raita for a perfect weekend dinner with family and friends.

Prep Time	:	20 Mins
Cooks Time	:	20 Mins
Total Time	:	40 Mins
Cuisine	:	North Indian
Serving	:	4 Servings

Equipments Used: Hard Anodised Kadai (Wok)

Ingredients

For the paneer stuffing

200 grams Paneer (Homemade Cottage Cheese) , cut into 1-inch cubes

2 Green Chilli , finely chopped

1 teaspoon Ginger , finely chopped

1 tablespoon Sultana Raisins

6 Cashew nuts , finely chopped

6 Whole Almonds (Badam) , finely chopped

6 Pistachios , finely chopped

1/4 teaspoon Turmeric powder (Haldi)

2 teaspoons Gram flour (besan)

Salt , to taste

1/4 teaspoon Cardamom Powder (Elaichi)

For the kofta gravy

1 teaspoon Oil

2 Bay leaf (tej patta)

2-3 Cardamom (Elaichi) Pods/Seeds

1 Cinnamon Stick (Dalchini)

2-3 Cloves (Laung)

1 Mace (Javitri)

1 Star anise

1 cup Homemade tomato puree

1 inch Ginger

3 cloves Garlic

1 Onion , roughly chopped

2 teaspoons Coriander Powder (Dhania)

1/2 teaspoon Red Chilli powder

1/4 teaspoon Turmeric powder (Haldi)

10 Cashew nuts , soaked and grind to a smooth paste

2 tablespoons Curd (Dahi / Yogurt)

Salt , to taste

1 tablespoon Kasuri Methi (Dried Fenugreek Leaves)

1 tablespoon Honey

1/2 cup Fresh cream

How to make Sweet & Spicy Stuffed Paneer In Kofta Curry Recipe

To begin making Stuffed Paneer In Kofta Curry Recipe, we will begin with the stuffing for the panner. Scoop out or cut out little paneer from the

center of each cube. You can use a melon scooper
or with a small spoon.

Transfer the scooped out paneer to a bowl, crumble
/ grate and set aside.

Heat oil in a heavy bottomed pan. Add finely
chopped green chillies and ginger, sauté until the
ginger is fragrant.

Add raisins and chopped nuts, sauté another 30
seconds. Add this mixture to crumbled paneer
along with turmeric powder, besan, salt and
cardamom powder. Mix well to come. Adjust the
salt according to taste.

Stuff this paneer and nut mixture in scooped out
paneer cubes and press firmly.

Heat a teaspoon of oil in a pan over medium heat.
Add the stuffed paneer pieces and pan fry the
paneer cubes until lightly golden on both sides.
Once done remove from the pan and keep aside.

To begin making the kofta curry, grind the onion,
ginger and garlic to a smooth paste. Keep aside.

Grind the cashew nuts along with a little water and
make a smooth paste. Keep aside.

Heat oil in a pan over medium heat; add the
whole spices and saute it for a few seconds until

you can smell the aromas coming through. Add the ginger garlic and onion paste and saute for about a minute until the raw smell goes away.

At this stage, add the turmeric powder, coriander powder, and red chilli powder. Adding the condiments to the onion ginger garlic paste helps further reduce the raw smell.

Saute for a few seconds and then add the tomato puree, cashew nut puree, salt to taste and the fresh cream. Add a little water to adjust the consistency of the kofta gravy.

Simmer this kofta curry for 3 to 4 minutes until the flavors combine well. Once done, turn off the heat, stir in the kasuri methi and check the salt and spices. Adjust to suit your taste.

Transfer the kofta curry to a serving bowl and when you are ready to serve, place the stuffed paneer in the curry and serve warm.

Serve your Stuffed Paneer Baskets with Punjabi Dal Tadka, Mixed Vegetable Pulao (Pilaf), Butter Garlic Naan, Kela Anar Raita for a perfect weekend dinner with family and friends.

Ginger Garlic Tofu Curry Recipe

Ginger Garlic Tofu Curry Recipe is a creamy coconut based curry with an Indian touch of turmeric powder and garam masala. This recipe is a perfect dish for your weekend dinners with your friends or family.

Serve Ginger Garlic Tofu Curry Recipe along with Steamed rice or Pudina Tawa Paratha for a weekday lunch or dinner.

Prep Time	:	15 Mins
Cooks Time	:	30 Mins
Total Time	:	45 Mins
Cuisine	:	Indian
Serving	:	2 Servings

Equipments Used: Hard Anodised Kadai (Wok)

Ingredients

150 grams Tofu , cubed

1 inch Ginger

3 Garlic , crushed

1 Carrot (Gajjar) , chopped

1/4 cup Spring Onion (Bulb & Greens) , whites, chopped

1/4 cup Spring Onion Greens , chopped

2 Green Chillies , chopped

1/4 cup Coconut milk

1/2 cup Vegetable stock

1/2 teaspoon Turmeric powder (Haldi)

Black pepper powder , according to your taste

1 teaspoon Garam masala powder

1 teaspoon Sweet and Spicy Red Chilli Sauce (Tomato Chilli Sauce)

Salt , to taste

1 teaspoon Soy sauce

1 teaspoon Corn flour , dissolved in 2 tablespoon water

How to make Ginger Garlic Tofu Curry Recipe

To begin making Ginger Garlic Tofu curry, heat 1 tablespoon of oil in a pan. Add crushed ginger and garlic and cook it till it turns golden brown.

Once it is done, add chopped spring onion whites, greens and chilies into the pan. Stir it well.

Add chopped carrot and mix it properly. Add turmeric powder, tomato chili sauce and pepper powder. make sure everything is mixed properly.

Add soya sauce, vegetable stock and coconut milk and stir everything nicely. Cover the pan and cook it for about 10 minutes. Add tofu cubes and salt according to your taste. Let it cook for about 10 minutes more.

Add corn flour dissolved water and cook for another 2 minutes. Switch off the heat and transfer it to a serving bowl.

Vegan Navratan Korma Recipe

The Vegan Navratan Korma Recipe is a rich gravy with vegetables, fruit, dry fruits and nuts with a delicate flavour and richness from all the nut paste and creamy yogurt. This is a great dish to make when you have special guests or when you are in a mood to pamper your family.

Serve the Vegan Navratan Korma along with a Paneer Pulao with Green Peas and Tadka Raita Recipe (Spiced Curd With Onions) to make a delicious weeknight dinner or even serve as a main course for parties.

Prep Time   :   60 Mins

Cooks Time   :   30 Mins

Total Time : 90 Mins

Cuisine : North Indian

Serving : 4 Servings

Equipments Used: Preethi Blue Leaf Mixer Grinder, Cast Iron Cooking Pot/ Casserole

Ingredients

2 Carrots (Gajjar) , diced small

10 to 12 Green beans (French Beans) , cut into 1 inch pieces

1/2 cup Cauliflower (gobi) , cut into florets

2 Potatoes (Aloo) , boiled and diced

1/2 cup Tofu , diced

2 Onions , sliced

6 Green Chillies

2 tablespoon Ginger Garlic Paste

1/2 teaspoon Turmeric powder (Haldi)

1/2 teaspoon Red Chilli powder

3-4 Cardamom (Elaichi) Pods/Seeds , powdered

1 Black cardamom (Badi Elaichi)

3 Cloves (Laung)

1 inch Ginger

1 cup Coconut Yogurt , optional

1/2 cup Coconut milk , thick

Mint Leaves (Pudina) , as needed

6-8 Saffron strands

Edible Silver Foil/Leaf (Chandi Ka Vark) , optional

Pineapple , few pieces

2 tablespoons Sultana Raisins

6-8 Cashew nuts , toasted

1 tablespoon Whole Almonds (Badam) , sliced

1 tablespoon Pistachios , sliced

1/2 Garam masala powder , optional

Coconut Oil , cold pressed, as needed

For the paste

1-1/2 tablespoons Poppy seeds

10 Cashew nuts , whole

15 Whole Almonds (Badam)

**How to make Vegan Navratan Korma Recipe**

To begin making the Vegan Navratan Korma, soak cashews and almonds reserved for the paste in water for 40 minutes. Grind this to a smooth paste along with poppy seeds and set aside.

Chop all the vegetables and gather all the ingredients required for the korma.Steam the vegetables with a pinch of salt until tender, make sure they hold the shape.

Grind the poppy seeds, cashew and almonds into a smooth paste, adding little water. Keep the nut-seed mixture aside.

In a large pan heat some oil, add cloves, cinnamon, green cardamom and black cardamom, now add sliced onions, ginger and garlic paste and saute the raw smell disappears, add green chillies and cook briefly. Let this mixture cool down to room temperature.

Now add these ingredients into a mixie jar and grind to smooth.

Return this gravy into the pan, add turmeric powder, red chilli powder and some salt and cook for 3-4 minutes.

Now to this mixture add the coconut yogurt, coconut milk and the nut-seed paste and mix to well and cook for 4-5 minutes or until the korma thickens.

Add the cooked vegetables, tofu and a cup of water and cook until the korma comes together. This should take around 4-5 minutes. Add little water to loosen the korma if required. Add salt and adjust the seasoning. Finally sprinkle the garam masala if using and give it a stir.

In a small pan, heat some coconut oil and gently fry cashews and sultanas, turn off the heat, add sliced almonds and pistachios and roast for a few seconds.

Spoon the Vegan Navratan Korma into a serving bowl, place the chandi ka warq if using, top it with cashews, sultanas, almonds and pistachios. Now arrange slices of pineapple, saffron and mint leaves on top.

Serve the Vegan Navratan Korma along with a Paneer Pulao with Green Peas and Tadka Raita Recipe (Spiced Curd With Onions) to make a delicious weeknight dinner or even serve as a main course for parties.

Bengali Style Kanch kolar Kofta Curry Recipe (Green Plantain Kofta Curry Recipe)

Bengali Style Kanch kolar Kofta Curry Recipe (Green Plantain Kofta Curry Recipe) is an all time favorite Bengali dish made with soft and crispy Koftas dipped in thin and tangy based curry. The Raw banana is a rich source of vitamins, minerals, and fiber. The starch content present in raw bananas will help in controlling blood sugar level and managing cholesterol.

Serve the Bengali Style Kanch kolar Kofta Curry Recipe (Green Plantain Kofta Curry Recipe) with hot Phulkas and steam rice.

Prep Time   :   10 Mins

Cooks Time   :   30 Mins

Total Time   :   40 Mins

Cuisine   :   Bengali

Serving   :   4 Servings

Equipments Used: Hard Anodized Pressure Cooker, Hard Anodised Kadai (Wok)

Ingredients

For the Koftas

1 Raw Banana

2 Potatoes (Aloo) , boiled

1 teaspoon Turmeric powder (Haldi)

2 teaspoon Panch Phoran Masala

2 teaspoon Red Chilli powder

For the gravy

1 Tomato

1 inch Ginger , grated

2 Green Chillies , finely chopped

2 teaspoon Cumin seeds (Jeera)

1/2 teaspoon Sugar

1 teaspoon Turmeric powder (Haldi)

2 teaspoon Cumin powder (Jeera)

1 teaspoon Garam masala powder

1/2 teaspoon Red Chilli powder

2 Bay leaf (tej patta)

2 sprig Coriander (Dhania) Leaves , chopped

How to make Bengali Style Kanch kolar Kofta Curry Recipe (Green Plantain Kofta Curry Recipe)

We begin making the Bengali Style Kanch kolar Kofta Curry Recipe (Green Plantain Kofta Curry Recipe) by boiling the peeled raw banana and potatoes in a pressure cooker for 4 whistles and releasing the pressure naturally.

In the meanwhile, heat the pan with oil and sauté the tomatoes till it is soft and mushy. Add salt and sprinkle little sugar to reduce the tanginess. Then let it cool down and grind the tomato into a puree consistency.

Once the potatoes and raw bananas are cooked, smash it along with all the masala powders and make it into a ball. Pan Fry them on the Kuzhi Paniyaram Pan till it is brown evenly. Keep it aside.

Heat a kadai with oil, add bay leaf and crackle cumin seeds, then add the tomato puree, add in all the spice powders mentioned in the gravy list. Add 1 cup of water and let it boil for about 15 minutes.

Once it thickens slightly add in the koftas and sprinkle with chopped coriander seeds.

Serve the Bengali Style Kanch kolar Kofta Curry Recipe (Green Plantain Kofta Curry Recipe) with hot Phulkas and steam rice.

Murungai Keerai Kollu Kuzhambu - Drumstick Leaves Horse Gram Curry

The Murungai Keerai Kollu Kuzhambu Recipe is a wholesome tangy curry that is made from horse gram dal and drumstick leaves - both of which being super foods for a healthy diet. Serve this curry along with a bowl of hot rice for a comforting weeknight dinner.

The Murungai Keerai Kollu Kuzhambu Recipe is a wholesome tangy curry that is made from horse gram dal and drumstick leaves - both of which being super foods for a healthy diet. Serve this curry along with a bowl of hot rice for a comforting weeknight dinner.

Chettinad cuisine is one of the most popular cuisines of Southern India, that is packed with a few essential ingredients and that is the baby onion and the black peppercorns. And this Kuzhambu is packed with flavors of just that.

Did you know: Drumstick leaves are known for their excellent source of nutrition and are a natural energy booster. Drumstick leaves also known as Moringa, helps lower blood pressure, blood sugar in diabetics and is also a sleep aid. Its detoxifying effect may come from Moringa's ability to purify water. Moringa acts as a coagulant attaching itself to harmful material and bacteria.

The Murungai Keerai Kollu Kuzhambu Recipe is a perfect dish to go along with some steaming hot rice, Cabbage Poriyal and Appalam. Serve it for lunch or dinner and you will surely enjoy this spicy curry.

Prep Time	:	10 Mins
Cooks Time	:	30 Mins
Total Time	:	40 Mins
Cuisine	:	Chettinad
Serving	:	4 Servings

Equipments Used: Hard Anodized Pressure Cooker, Small Skillet (Shallow Fry Pan/ Omelette Pan)

Ingredients

1 cup Horse Gram Dal (Kollu/ Kulith) , soaked for 3 to 4 hours

2 cups Drumstick Leaves (Moringa/Murungai Keerai) , roughly chopped

1 cups Tamarind Water

10 Pearl onions (Sambar Onions) , peeled and halved

2 Tomatoes , roughly chopped

1 teaspoon Sambar Powder

1 teaspoon Whole Black Peppercorns , coarsely pounded

Salt , to taste

1 teaspoon Jaggery

Ingredients for seasoning

1 teaspoon Sesame (Gingelly) Oil

1 teaspoon Mustard seeds (Rai/ Kadugu)

1/2 teaspoon Methi Seeds (Fenugreek Seeds)

2 sprig Curry leaves , roughly torn

How to make Murungai Keerai Kollu Kuzhambu - Drumstick Leaves Horse Gram Curry

To begin making the Murungai Keerai Kollu Kuzhambu Recipe, first get all the ingredients prepped and ready. Make the tamarind water according to the recipe - How To Make Tamarind Water.

Soak the horse gram for a couple of hours. Soaking helps it to cook faster.

Pressure cook the drumstick leaves, along with salt and 2 tablespoons of water for just 1 whistle. Release the pressure immediately, to prevent overcooking the greens and also to retain its fresh green colour.

Once the ingredients are prepped, we will cook them all in the pressure cooker. Into the pressure cooker, add a teaspoon of oil - saute the onions until lightly tender.

Once the onions are tender, add the horse gram, tomatoes, tamarind water, salt, jaggery, sambar powder, pepper and salt. Stir well to combine and cook for 6 to 8 whistles.

After 8 whistles, turn off the heat and allow the pressure to release naturally. Once released, stir in the cooked Murungai Keerai into the Kollu Kuzhambu.

Give the Murungai Keerai Kollu Kuzhambu a brisk boil and turn off the heat.

The Kuzhambu will be a little runny, if you like a thicker, then you can simmer the Kuzhambu on low heat until it thickens.

Check the salt and spices and adjust to suit your taste.

The final step is the seasoning. Heat a little oil in a small tadka pan, add the mustard seeds, fenugreek seeds and allow it to crackle. Once it crackles add the curry leaves and stir.

Turn off the heat and add the seasoning to the Murungai Keerai Kollu Kuzhambu and serve.

The Murungai Keerai Kollu Kuzhambu Recipe is a perfect dish to go along with some steaming hot rice, Cabbage Poriyal and Appalam. Serve it for lunch or dinner and you will surely enjoy this spicy curry.

Mambazha Mor Kuzhambu Recipe - Ripe Mango Mor Kuzhambu

Give this Mambazha Mor Kuzhambu a try for lunch, it is made from ripe mangoes cooked in a spicy coconut and curd gravy. Serve the Kuzhambu along with Steamed Rice, Chow Chow Thoran and Elai Vadam for lunch or dinner.

Mambazha Mor Kuzhambu is a delicious mango curry made from ripe mangoes simmered in a delicious coconut and yogurt based gravy. The Mor Kuzhambu is also popularly known as Pulissery in Kerala and is often made with a variety of vegetables like ripe bananas, ash gourd, capsicum, drumstick, lady's finger and carrots used either just as one vegetable or as a combination of 2 vegetables.

Serve Mambazha Mor Kuzhambu Recipe along with Steamed Rice, Chow Chow Thoran and Elai Vadam for a weekday meal.

Prep Time	:	15 Mins
Cooks Time	:	15 Mins
Total Time	:	30 Mins
Cuisine	:	South Indian
Serving	:	4 Servings

Equipments Used: Hard Anodised Kadai (Wok), Tadka Pan (Seasoning Pan)

Ingredients

1 Mango (Ripe) , peeled and chopped into big pieces

1/4 teaspoon Turmeric powder (Haldi)

1/4 cup Fresh coconut

1 teaspoon Cumin seeds (Jeera)

1 Green Chilli , or fry red chilli

1 cup Curd (Dahi / Yogurt)

Salt , to taste

For Seasoning/ Tadka

1 teaspoon Coconut Oil

1/2 teaspoon Mustard seeds (Rai/ Kadugu)

1/2 teaspoon Methi Seeds (Fenugreek Seeds)

1 sprig Curry leaves , as required

How to make Mambazha Mor Kuzhambu Recipe - Ripe Mango Mor Kuzhambu

To begin making the Mambazha Mor Kuzhambu recipe, prep all the ingredients and keep it ready.

The first step is to make a paste of the coconut mixture. Into a mixer grinder, add the coconut, cumin seeds, green chillies, salt and grind it along with 1/2 cup of warm water into a smooth paste.

Warm water helps to blend the coconut into a much smoother mixture.

Into a sauce pan, add the mangoes, coconut mixture, turmeric powder and water. Adjust the consistency of the gravy such that you have a thick pouring consistency.

Give the Mambazha Mor Kuzhambu a brisk boil for about 3 to 3 minutes and turn off the heat. Check the salt and adjust to taste accordingly.

For the tadka, preheat a tadka pan over medium heat; add the oil and allow it to get warm.

Once the oil is warm, add the mustard seeds and fenugreek seeds to allow it to crackle. Stir in the curry leaves and turn off the heat.

Pour this seasoning over the Mambazha Mor Kuzhambu and give it a stir. Transfer the Mambazha Mor Kuzhambu to a serving bowl and serve hot.

Serve Mambazha Mor Kuzhambu along with Steamed Rice, Chow Chow Thoran and Elai Vadam for a weekday meal.

Kollu Puli Kuzhambu Recipe - Horsegram In A Tangy Gravy

Kollu Puli Kuzhambu Recipe is a tangy and delicious Kuzhambu recipe of Horse Gram Dal prepared in a unique way. Serve it with Steamed Rice and Poriyal for a weekday lunch.

Kollu Puli Kuzhambu, is a horse gram recipe which is traditionally made in an earthenware pot. Shallots added to the gravy gives a unique flavour and makes it a great dish that can be eaten with a variety of other dishes.

Did you know: Horsegram is a lentil variety that is loaded with dietary fiber, vitamins, iron etc. Intake of Horse gram is excellent for people who are trying to reduce their weight. Horse Gram helps in curing bladder stone issues and also in improving the digestive system. Most important of all, it is great for Diabetics.

Serve Kollu Puli Kuzhambu along with hot Steamed Rice, Carrot Poriyal and Elai Vadam for a comforting weekday lunch.

You can also serve Kollu Puli Kuzhambu along with Ragi Mudde for a super healthy lunch for Diabetics.

Prep Time	:	40 Mins
Cooks Time	:	40 Mins
Total Time	:	80 Mins

Cuisine : Tamil Nadu

Serving : 6 Servings

Equipments Used: Preethi Blue Leaf Mixer Grinder, Hard Anodised Kadai (Wok), Tadka Pan (Seasoning Pan)

Ingredients

100 grams Horse Gram Dal (Kollu/ Kulith)

200 grams Shallots , 100 grams for chutney + 100 for the Kuzhambu

1 Tomato

1/2 cup Fresh coconut , grated

2 tablespoons Coriander (Dhania) Seeds

10 Dry Red Chillies , 5 for the chutney + 5 for the Kuzhambu

5 cloves Garlic

2 sprig Curry leaves

1 teaspoon Cumin seeds (Jeera)

1 teaspoon Whole Black Peppercorns

Salt , according to your taste

1/2 teaspoon Asafoetida (hing)

1/2 teaspoon Turmeric powder (Haldi)

2 cups Tamarind Water

3 teaspoons Gingelly oil

1 teaspoon Mustard seeds (Rai/ Kadugu)

How to make Kollu Puli Kuzhambu Recipe - Horse Gram In A Tangy Gravy

To begin making the Kollu Puli Kuzhambu, soak horse gram dal in a sufficient amount of water for a couple of hours.

After 2 hours, pressure cook horse gram along with 1 chopped tomato, salt and the required water.

Pressure cook for 4 whistles, turn the heat to low and simmer for 20 minutes. Turn off the heat, allowing the pressure to release naturally.

Once the pressure has released naturally, open the pressure cooker and drain the horse gram and set aside. Reserve the water for the gravy.

Place a heavy bottomed pan on low heat and add 1 teaspoon of oil.

Once the oil is hot, add peppercorns, cumin seeds, coriander seeds and 5 dry red chillies.

Roast all the ingredients for 4 to 6 minutes, until you can smell the aroma of the spices.

Once they are roasted, add a few curry leaves, peeled shallots, grated coconut, garlic and continue to saute till the onions become soft.

Add in the cooked horse gram with tomato. Stir all the ingredients well and turn off the flame.

Allow the ingredients to cool and grind to chutney consistency with adequate salt.

Kollu chutney or horse gram chutney is ready. The process of making this into a puli kuzhambu starts from here. This chutney is the base for the Puli Kuzhambu.

To make the Puli Kuzhambu, in a bowl, add the prepared tamarind water, the ground kollu tomato chutney along with the water it was cooked in. The kuzhambu should be thin.

Slice the remaining shallots and break the remaining chillies into pieces.

In an earthenware pot, add 2 teaspoons of oil and add the shallots, broken red chillies, turmeric powder and asafoetida.

Alternatively if you do not have an earthenware pot, use it in a saucepan.

Once the onion turns pink, add the tamarind horse gram kuzhambu mixture and simmer for 15 minutes till the gravy thickens and the raw smell of tamarind goes away.

Meanwhile in a tadka or tempering pan, add a teaspoon of oil. Once the oil is hot, add mustard seeds. Add 2 finely chopped shallots and fry till they are golden brown.

Now add the curry leaves and turn off the tadka pan.

Pour the tempering over the Kollu Puli Kuzhambu and turn off the heat. Your tangy Kollu Puli Kuzhambu is ready to be served.

Serve Kollu Puli Kuzhambu along with hot Steamed Rice, Carrot Poriyal and Elai Vadam for a comforting weekday lunch.

You can also serve Kollu Puli Kuzhambu along with Ragi Mudde for a super healthy lunch for Diabetics.

Kathiri Urulai Masala Kuzhambu Recipe - Brinjal And Potato Masala Gravy

Kathiri Urulai Masala Kuzhambu is a South Indian gravy which is made with potatoes and brinjal cooked in a tomato tamarind gravy. Serve this

Kuzhambu along with steamed rice for a delicious weeknight meal.

Kathiri Urulai Masala Kuzhambu is a simple gravy where Brinjal and Potatoes are cooked in an onion tomato tamarind gravy along with ground coconut and spices like fennel and khus khus, which gives a nice flavour and taste.

This is a rich gravy recipe and will make for a heavy meal so, this dish can be wisely paired with any South Indian tiffin item for a heavy breakfast.

Serve Kathiri Urulai Masala Kuzhambu along with any South Indian Breakfast Item like Idli, Dosa, Kerala Parotta or even serve for dinner along with Steamed Rice and Beetroot Raita.

Prep Time	:	10 Mins
Cooks Time	:	30 Mins
Total Time	:	40 Mins
Cuisine	:	South Indian
Serving	:	4 Servings

Equipments Used: Hard Anodised Kadai (Wok), Preethi Zodiac 750-Watt Mixer Grinder

Ingredients

2 Brinjal (Baingan / Eggplant) , diced

1 Potato (Aloo) , diced

20 grams Tamarind , gooseberry sized

1 Onion , finely chopped

1 Tomato , finely chopped

1 teaspoon Red Chilli powder

1/4 teaspoon Turmeric powder (Haldi)

1/4 cup Fresh coconut , grated

1 teaspoon Fennel seeds (Saunf)

1 teaspoon Khus Khus

5 Cashew nuts

4 Dry Red Chillies

1 teaspoon Mustard seeds (Rai/ Kadugu)

1 inch Cinnamon Stick (Dalchini)

1 sprig Curry leaves

1 tablespoon Oil

Salt , as per your taste

Water , as needed

How to make Kathiri Urulai Masala Kuzhambu Recipe - Brinjal And Potato Masala Gravy

To begin making Kathiri Urulai Masala Kuzhambu, soak tamarind in 1 cup of hot water and extract its pulp. Keep aside.

Heat a tablespoon of oil in a heavy bottomed pan. Once the oil is hot, add mustard seeds.

When mustard seeds crackle, add cinnamon stick and curry leaves. Sauté it for a minute.

After a minute, add chopped onion and sauté it till onion turns soft and translucent.

Add in the sliced brinjal and potato, mix, cover the pan with a lid until the potatoes and brinjals are half cooked. This will take about 3 to 4 minutes.

Now, add finely chopped tomatoes and cook till the tomatoes turn mushy. Finally, add in tamarind pulp, turmeric powder, red chilli powder and salt. Let it cook for 3 to 4 minutes.

Meanwhile, take grated coconut, khus khus, fennel seeds, cashews and red chillies in a mixer jar. Grind it to a smooth paste.

Add this paste to the gravy. Boil it for 2-3 minutes. Turn off the heat and Kathiri Urulai Masala Kuzhambu Recipe is ready to be served.

Serve Kathiri Urulai Masala Kuzhambu along with any South Indian Breakfast Item like Idli, Dosa, Kerala Parotta or even serve for dinner along with Rotis or Steamed Rice and Beetroot Raita.

Orange Peel Kuzhambu Recipe - Orange Peel Tamarind Based Curry

Orange Peel Kuzhambu is a delicious Kuzhambu recipe which is made with orange peels and tamarind. This South Indian Style Curry makes for a delicious curry along with Steamed Rice and Keerai Kootu for a weekday lunch.

Orange Peel Kuzhambu is a spicy, tangy gravy made with tamarind juice and orange peels. Most of us just throw away the orange peel after eating the orange. But the orange peel tastes amazing and h s a host of health benefits.

So next time you want to make any South Indian vegetarian curry for a weekday meal, do try this curry where you can use the orange peels remaining from your orange.

Orange peels are a source of health-promoting carbohydrates and this is a great way to include it in your diet.

Serve Orange Peel Kuzhambu along with Steaming Hot Rice & Keerai Kootu for a delicious lunch. You can also serve this Kuzhambu along with Pongal, Dosa, Idli or Upma.

Prep Time	:	10 Mins
Cooks Time	:	20 Mins
Total Time	:	30 Mins
Cuisine	:	South Indian
Serving	:	4 Servings

Equipments Used: Hard Anodised Kadai (Wok)

**Ingredients**

1/3 cup Orange peel , finely chopped

1 inch Ginger , thinly sliced

1 Green Chilli , slit lengthwise

1 cup Tamarind Paste

2 tablespoon Sambar Powder

2 tablespoon Jaggery

1/4 teaspoon Turmeric powder (Haldi)

1/4 teaspoon Asafoetida (hing)

1 cup Water

Salt , as per your taste

2 tablespoons Sesame (Gingelly) Oil

1 teaspoon Mustard seeds (Rai/ Kadugu)

1 sprig Curry leaves

How to make Orange Peel Kuzhambu Recipe - Orange Peel Tamarind Based Curry

To begin making the Orange Peel Kuzhambu Recipe, heat a teaspoon of oil in a kadai over medium heat.

Once the oil is hot, add mustard seeds. Once the seeds splutter, add slit green chillies, sliced ginger and curry leaves. Saute it for about 30 seconds.

Then, add the chopped Orange peel and saute for a few minutes until the orange peels shrivel.

Next, add salt, sambar powder, turmeric powder, asafoetida and stir everything well until the sambar powder gets coated well on the orange peel. This will take about 2 to 3 minutes.

Once done, stir in the tamarind juice and add jaggery to it. Add 1 cup water and allow it to boil for 5 minutes on a rolling boil.

Once the water has reduced to half the quantity and the gravy is thickened, you can switch off the flame. This would take 15 - 20 minutes.

Orange Peel Kuzhambu is ready to be served.

Serve Orange Peel Kuzhambu along with Steaming Hot Rice & Keerai Kootu for a sumptuous lunch. You can also serve this kuzhambu along with Pongal, Dosa, Idli or Upma.

Tirunelveli Sodhi Kuzhambu Recipe - Mixed Vegetable Stew

A Tirunelveli Kuzhambu recipe called Sodhi Kuzhambu that is prepared in a coconut milk gravy and cooked along with an assortment of seasonal vegetables. Serve it along with any South Indian breakfast item as a side dish.

Sodhi Kuzhambu or better known as "Mappillai Sodhi" in Tirunelveli area of Tamilnadu. Mappillai means bridegroom in tamil and this coconut milk based curry is prepared by the bride's family to treat their son in law on the first visit to the bride's place after marriage. The curry is so mild and full of wonderful flavor, goes well with rice, idli dosa, idiyappam typically with almost all South Indian breakfast items.

Serve the Sodhi Kuzhambu for a special occasion and serve along with Puri or Steamed Rice and Inji chutney for a delicious meal.

Prep Time	:	20 Mins
Cooks Time	:	25 Mins
Total Time	:	45 Mins
Cuisine	:	Tamil Nadu
Serving	:	4 Servings

Equipments Used: Hard Anodized Pressure Cooker, Preethi Turbo Chop

Ingredients

1/4 cup Yellow Moong Dal (Split) , washed and kept aside

1 Potato (Aloo) , cut into small pieces

8 Green beans (French Beans) , cut into small pieces

1 Carrot (Gajjar) , cut into small pieces

1/4 cup Green peas (Matar)

1/2 cup Cauliflower (gobi) , florets

2 Drumstick , cut into 1 inch pieces, cut lengthwise

5 Pearl onions (Sambar Onions) , cut into half

1 Tomato , cut into quarters

1/4 teaspoon Mustard seeds (Rai/ Kadugu)

1 teaspoon Cumin seeds (Jeera)

1 tablespoon Oil

1/4 teaspoon Asafoetida (hing)

1 tablespoon Lemon juice

1 cup Fresh coconut , grated

1 inch Ginger

7 cloves Garlic

4 Green Chillies , slit

1 sprig Curry leaves

Coriander (Dhania) Leaves , for garnish

Salt , as per taste

How to make Tirunelveli Sodhi Kuzhambu Recipe - Mixed Vegetable Stew

To begin making Tirunelveli Sodhi Kuzhambu, into a pressure cooker, add the chopped cauliflower florets, potatoes, green beans, carrots, drumsticks and peas. Add a pinch of asafoetida along with 1/4 cup water.

Pressure cook the vegetables for 2 whistles and release the pressure immediately by running the pressure cooker under running water.

Open the lid and transfer the cooked vegetables into a bowl. This is done in order to keep the nutrition and colour of the vegetables.

In the same pressure cooker at 1/4 cup moong dal along with 1/4 cup water. Pressure cook for 3-4 whistles and turn off the pressure cooker. Release the pressure naturally.

In the small jar of a mixer, add green chillies, ginger, 5 cloves of garlic and grind to a smooth paste. Set aside.

*__To prepare the coconut milk__

Next add the coconut and grind into a coarse mixture.Then add 1/2 cup of water and grind into a smooth paste. Transfer the coconut paste into a strainer and extract the coconut milk. That's the thick coconut milk.

In the same jar, add the extracted coconut again with 3/4 cup of water and grind into smooth paste.Extract through the strainer and discard the coconut residue. This is thin coconut milk.

To make the Kuzhambu

Heat a kadai with 1 tablespoon of oil on medium flame. Once the oil is hot, add mustard seeds & cumin seeds

Once the mustard starts sputtering, add the chopped onions, remaining garlic cloves and curry leaves. Saute until the onions and garlic become translucent.

Next add in the ginger, garlic chilli paste and saute until the raw smell goes away.

Add in the chopped tomatoes and cook until the tomatoes turn mushy.

Now add in the pressure cooked vegetables and moong dal into the kadai. Mix well.

Once all the ingredients are mixed well, add the thin coconut milk and let it simmer on a low flame for a few minutes.

Finally add the thick coconut milk and mix well. Let it be on a flame for 3 mins & switch off the flame.

Finally add the coriander leaves and lemon juice & mix well. Your Sodhi Kuzhambu is ready to be served.

Make Sodhi Kuzhambu for a special occasion and serve along with Puri or Steamed Rice and Inji chutney for a delicious meal.

Sorakkai Kozhukattai Paal Kuzhambu Recipe - Bottle Gourd Curry

Sorakkai Kozhukattai Paal Kuzhambu Recipe is a delicious combination of bottle gourd and rice flour balls cooked in a coconut and milk gravy and tempered with mustard seeds and urad dal. Serve it with Steamed Rice and Elai Vadam.

Sorakkai Kozhukattai Paal Kuzhambu is an authentic recipe from Tamil Nadu. It is a mildly spiced curry with coconut and tiny rice dumplings (kozhukattai) that are cooked along with bottle gourd. Sugar is added to give a little sweet taste .Tiny rice dumplings and chopped bottle gourd gives a nice texture to the curry. As it is mildly spiced we can pair it up with any tangy and spicy gravies like puli kuzhambu for lunch.

Serve Sorakkai Kozhukattai Paal Kuzhambu along with Steamed Rice or even Phulkas for a wholesome lunch.

Prep Time	:	15 Mins
Cooks Time	:	35 Mins
Total Time	:	50 Mins
Cuisine	:	Tamil Nadu
Serving	:	4 Servings

Equipments Used: Hard Anodized Pressure Cooker, Hard Anodised Kadai (Wok)

Ingredients

1 Bottle gourd (lauki) , cut into small pieces

1/4 cup Rice flour

2 tablespoons Chana dal (Bengal Gram Dal)

1/2 cup Fresh coconut , grated

1/4 cup Milk

1/2 teaspoon Mustard seeds (Rai/ Kadugu)

1 teaspoon White Urad Dal (Split)

4 Dry Red Chillies

2 tablespoons Sugar

2 teaspoon Oil

Salt , as per your taste

Water , as needed

How to make Sorakkai Kozhukattai Paal Kuzhambu Recipe - Bottle Gourd Curry

To begin making Sorakkai Kozhukattai Paal Kuzhambu, first keep the chana dal soaked in warm water for 30 minutes.

To make the Kozhukattai Or Rice Flour Balls

In a saucepan, boil 1 cup of water. Once the water has boiled, add rice flour and mix well so that there are no lumps. Rice flour thickens quite quickly, so be sure to continuously stir.

Once the temperature of the rice and water mixture is cool enough to handle, make oval/round sized balls of 1/2 inch size - small Kozhukattai and keep aside.

To make the Paal Kuzhambu

In a pressure cooker, add the diced bottle gourd along with salt, 1/2 cup water and a pinch of turmeric.

Pressure cook the Sorakkai /bottle gourd for 2 whistles and release the pressure immediately by running the pressure cooker under water. Open the lid and keep aside.

Place a heavy bottomed pan on medium heat, add the soaked chana dal along with the soaked water. Since the chana dal has been soaked in warm water, it will be half cooked.

Add the cooked sorakkai/bottle gourd pieces, along with the cooked water

When dal gets half cooked add bottle gourd pieces along with the cooked water.

Next add the prepared kozhukattai in small quantities at a time and let it cook for 10 minutes on a medium flame.

Kozhukattais can stick in the bottom, if there is not enough water, so adjust the water quantity accordingly.

When kozhukattai gets cooked add grated coconut to it and stir it well.

Add in the sugar, milk and cook it for 2 more minutes and switch off the stove. (Instead of adding plain milk, you can also mix 1 tablespoon of rice flour with milk and add it to a curry to give thicker consistency)

For the tempering

In a tadka pan, heat 2 teaspoons of oil. Once the oil is hot, add mustard seeds.

When mustard seeds crackle, add urad dal and red chillies, saute until urad dal turns brown.

Pour this tadka/tempering to our prepared Pal Kuzhambu and your Sorakkai Kozhukattai Paal Kuzhambu is ready to be served.

Serve Sorakkai Kozhukattai Paal Kuzhambu along with Steamed Rice or even Phulkas for a wholesome lunch.

White Pumpkin Mor Kuzhambu Recipe - Kerala Style White Pumpkin Curry

White Pumpkin Mor Kuzhambu is a classic Kerala dish that is prepared with ground coconut and green chillies in curd. Serve this delicious Kuzhambu along with rice and a vendakka thoran for a simple weekday lunch.

This recipe of Kerala Style White Pumpkin Mor Kuzhambu is a classic Kerala dish that is a sure dish that is prepared at least one day a week. The simplicity of the dish and the number of ingredients with which it can be made is one of the reasons it is prepared so often.

Mor Kuzhambu is a recipe that is prepared with ground coconut and green chillies which is then mixed in whisked curd along with a seasonal vegetable. In this recipe, we have used white pumpkin or pushnikai or elavan (as it is called in Kerala) which is a water rich vegetable, and easy to digest.

Serve Mor Kuzhambu with Steamed Rice and Menthia Keerai Paruppu Usili for a simple weekday lunch.

Prep Time	:	10 Mins
Cooks Time	:	25 Mins
Total Time	:	35 Mins
Cuisine	:	Kerala
Serving	:	2 Servings

Equipments Used: Hard Anodized Pressure Cooker, Hard Anodised Kadai (Wok), Tadka Pan (Seasoning Pan), Preethi Zodiac 750-Watt Mixer Grinder

Ingredients

1-1/2 cups Curd (Dahi / Yogurt) , thick

1/2 cup Fresh coconut

1 cup Vellai Poosanikai (Ash gourd/White Pumpkin) , cubed

4 Green Chillies

1/4 teaspoon Black pepper powder

1/3 cup Water

1/4 teaspoon Turmeric powder (Haldi)

Salt , as per your taste

To Temper

1 teaspoon Coconut Oil

1/4 teaspoon Mustard seeds (Rai/ Kadugu)

1/4 teaspoon Methi Seeds (Fenugreek Seeds)

1 sprig Curry leaves

1 Dry Red Chilli

How to make White Pumpkin Mor Kuzhambu Recipe - Kerala Style White Pumpkin Curry

To begin making White Pumpkin Mor Kuzhambu, we need to first cook the pumpkin.

Pressure cook the white pumpkin with little water in a pressure cooker for 2 whistles and release the pressure immediately by running the cooker under cold water. Keep aside.

Meanwhile, whisk curd with water in a bowl until it's smooth. Make sure that there are no lumps in the curd.

Next, add grated coconut, green chilli, black pepper powder in a mixer grinder and grind it to a smooth paste with a little water. Your Kuzhambu paste is ready.

Transfer this kuzhambu paste to the curd and mix well. Once it is mixed properly, add in turmeric powder, cooked white pumpkin, salt and mix everything well.

Place this mixture on low heat in a saucepan and allow the mixture to become warm. You will notice a light froth around the edges of the vessel. Do not let the mixture boil, the curd will split on high heat.

Turn off the flame the moment you see froth. The next step is to temper the kuzhambu.

In a tempering pan/tadka pan, add one teaspoon of coconut oil. Once the oil is hot, add mustard seeds and fenugreek seeds,

Once the mustard seeds start to crackle, add the curry leaves, dry red chilli and give it a mix.

Turn off the flame and add this tempering to the Mor Kuzhambu. Your Mor Kuzhambu is ready to be served.

Serve Mor Kuzhambu with Steamed Rice and Menthia Keerai Paruppu Usili for a simple weekday lunch.

Notes

Do not boil the curd. It will curdle if you boil. Remove immediately after it starts frothing.

Whisk the curd and water to a uniform mixture, Lumps might lead to curdling while heating.

Always mix the veggies, grounded mixture to curd and then heat.

Apart from white pumpkin you can use colocasia, yam, plantains or ladies fingers.

Kondai Kadalai Puli Kuzhambu Recipe -Tangy South Indian Kala Chana Curry

Kondai Kadalai Puli Kuzhambu Recipe is a delicious South Indian Curry where Black Chickpeas are cooked in Tamarind Gravy. Serve it with Beetroot Thoran, Keerai Sambar and Steamed Rice for a weekday lunch or dinner.

Kondai Kadalai Puli Kuzhambu Recipe is a Black Chickpea Curry which is cooked in tamarind gravy.

It is different from kerala kadala curry and North Indian chole. Its flavour and taste is unique. It pairs well with hot steaming rice, paratha and it also goes well with idli/dosa.

As Chickpeas are high in protein, this gravy is healthy and delicious at the same time. It can be packed for a lunch box too as it is wholesome food. Black Chickpeas are also high in dietary fiber, rich in vitamins and minerals, packed with protein and low in fat and hence making it a diabetic friendly food. These beans may help lower your risk for cancer, heart disease and diabetes, as well as limiting increases in blood sugar levels after meals.

The Kondai Kadalai Puli Kuzhambu, is a wholesome diabetic friendly recipe that is packed with south indian flavors. Include it along with your main course for a diabetic friendly meal.

Serve Kondai Kadalai Puli Kuzhambu Recipe along with Beetroot Thoran, Keerai Sambar and Steamed Rice for lunch or dinner.

Prep Time	:	15 Mins
Cooks Time	:	30 Mins
Total Time	:	45 Mins
Cuisine	:	South Indian

Serving   :   3 Servings

Equipments Used: Hard Anodised Kadai (Wok)

Ingredients

1/2 cup Kala Chana (Brown Chickpeas)

30 grams Tamarind

3 teaspoons Sambar Powder

2 teaspoons Jaggery , powdered

1/2 teaspoon Mustard seeds (Rai/ Kadugu)

1/4 teaspoon Methi Seeds (Fenugreek Seeds)

1 tablespoon Sesame (Gingelly) Oil

14 cup Fresh coconut , grated

1 sprig Curry leaves

Salt , to taste

Water , as required

How to make Kondai Kadalai Puli Kuzhambu Recipe -Tangy South Indian Kala Chana Curry

To begin making the Kondai Kadalai Puli Kuzhambu Recipe, first wash and soak black chickpeas in enough water for about 8 to 10 hours or overnight.

Next add the black chickpeas/Kondai Kadalai in a pressure cooker along with required water and pressure cook it till the cooker releases 8 to 10 whistles over medium heat. Let the pressure release naturally.

It will take a good 20 minutes to cook the kala chana/ Kondai Kadalai in the pressure cooker.

Meanwhile, soak tamarind in hot water for 10 minutes and extract juice from it by adding water. You will get approximately 1-1/2 cups of water.

In a mixer grinder, blend the coconut, by adding 1/4 cup of warm water and make a smooth paste. Keep this aside.

Next, heat a heavy bottomed pan with a tablespoon of oil. Add mustard seeds, fenugreek seeds and let it roast for about 10 seconds and allow it to crackle.

After 10 seconds, add in the tamarind juice, curry leaves, sambar powder and salt. Allow the Puli Kuzhambu mixture to come to a brisk boil for 3 to 4 minutes.

Once it starts boiling, add the cooked chickpeas/ Kondai Kadalai, jaggery and coconut paste . Add salt to taste and let it cook for about 5 minutes.

If you want a thicker consistency of the Kondai Kadalai Puli Kuzhambu Recipe, cook for some more time with the pan open. Once done, check the salt to taste and adjust accordingly and serve hot.

Serve Kondai Kadalai Puli Kuzhambu along with Beetroot Thoran, Keerai Sambar and Steamed Rice for a weekday meal for lunch or dinner or even a diabetic friendly meal.

Kathirikai Sundakkai Vathal Kuzhambu Recipe

Here is a delicious Chettinad Vatha Kuzhambu made with sundakkai (turkey berries) and brinjal cooked in a tangy and sweet sauce of tamarind and jaggery along with a perfect blend of homemade spices. Serve it along with hot steamed rice, ghee and a poriyal for lunch or dinner.

The Kathirikai Sundakkai Vathal Kuzhambu Recipe is a delicious Chettinad style tangy gravy which is simmered along with tamarind, jaggery, homemade spices and along with sundakkai and brinjal.

Vatha meaning dried is a common ingredient that is added in Kuzhambu in Tamil Nadu and the common kind of Vatha that are used in Kuzhambus are Manathakkali, Veppam Poo and Appalam. It is traditionally called Kuzhambu when tamarind pulp and spices are combined and cooked with dried (vatha) ingredients and sometimes with seasonal vegetables.

Serve this delicious Kathirikai Sundakkai Vathal Kuzhambu along with Hot Steamed Rice,

Capsicum Masala Poriyal Recipe and Elai Vadam for an elaborate Tamilnadu Style lunch.

Prep Time	:	5 Mins
Cooks Time	:	30 Mins
Total Time	:	35 Mins
Cuisine	:	Chettinad
Serving	:	4 Servings

Equipments Used: Preethi Blue Leaf Mixer Grinder, Hard Anodised Kadai (Wok)

Ingredients

2 tablespoons Sundakkai (Turkey Berries)

2 tablespoons Sesame (Gingelly) Oil

1/2 teaspoon Mustard seeds (Rai/ Kadugu)

1/4 teaspoon Methi Seeds (Fenugreek Seeds)

2 sprig Curry leaves

1/4 teaspoon Asafoetida (hing)

12 Pearl onions (Sambar Onions) , peeled and quartered

6 Brinjal (Baingan / Eggplant) , quartered and soaked in salt water

50 grams Tamarind , soaked in water

2 tablespoons Sambar Powder , homemade

1 cup Water

1 tablespoon Jaggery

Salt , to taste

How to make Kathirikai Sundakkai Vathal Kuzhambu Recipe

To begin making Kathirikai Sundakkai Vathal Kuzhambu, prep all the ingredients and keep ready.

Extract the tamarind water, until you get 2 cups of tamarind water from the soaked tamarind. Keep this aside.

Heat oil in a pan over medium heat; add the sundakkai and roast until it is dark brown in colour and crisp. Once roasted, keep the sundakkai to the side.

Preheat oil in a pan over medium heat, add the mustard seeds and fenugreek seeds. Allow it to crackle.

Add the curry leaves, asafoetida, onion and brinjal (drain the water it was soaked in). Saute the onion and brinjal until the onion is roasted and brinjal is cooked and roasted. Cover the pan so the brinjal cooks faster.

Once done, add the roasted sundakkai, tamarind water, water, homemade sambar powder, jaggery and salt. Simmer the Kathirikai Sundakkai Vathal Kuzhambu for 15 to 20 minutes until the raw taste from the tamarind goes away and the vathal kuzhambu has thickened.

Give the Kathirikai Sundakkai Vathal Kuzhambu a stir occasionally so that the gravy does not stick to the bottom. Once done, check the taste and adjust the salt and spices accordingly. Turn off the heat and transfer the Kathirikai Sundakkai Vathal Kuzhambu to a serving bowl and serve hot.

Serve this delicious Kathirikai Sundakkai Vathal Kuzhambu along with Hot Steamed Rice,

Capsicum Masala Poriyal Recipe and Elai Vadam
for a delicious Tamilnadu Style lunch.

Thandu Keerai Puli Kuzhambu Recipe - Amaranth Greens in Tangy Curry

Thandu Keerai Puli Kuzhambu is a delicious gravy
with foxtail amaranth leaves that is cooked in a
tamarind gravy that can be served along with rice
and poriyal of your choice.

Thandu Keerai Puli Kuzhambu Recipe is a
traditional Tamil Nadu Style tamarind based curry
made with shallots or normal onion, sometimes with
garlic and vegetables. It pairs well with the lentil

based Kootus. Thandu Keerai Puli Kuzhambu Recipe is simple to make and therefore you can include them into your everyday meals.

The curry is spiced with roasted fenugreek seeds powder and sambar powder, which enhances the flavour of gravy. The addition of onion and garlic cloves adds a nice crunch to the dish. Also, make sure you use sesame oil to cook the Puli Kuzhambu, it enhances the flavour and taste.

Serve Thandu Keerai Puli Kuzhambu Recipe along with Steamed Rice, Kathirikai Kootu, Carrot and Beans Poriyal Recipe and Curd for a Weeknight dinner.

Prep Time   :   10 Mins

Cooks Time   :   20 Mins

Total Time   :   30 Mins

Cuisine   :   South Indian

Serving   :   4 Servings

Equipments Used: Hard Anodised Kadai (Wok)

Ingredients

1 cup Green Amaranth Leaves , roughly chopped

20 grams Tamarind , soaked in hot water and pulp extracted

1 Onion , finely chopped

1 Tomato , roughly chopped

10 cloves Garlic

1 teaspoon Mustard seeds (Rai/ Kadugu)

1/4 teaspoon Asafoetida (hing)

1 sprig Curry leaves

2 teaspoons Sambar Powder

1 teaspoon Methi Powder (Fenugreek Powder)

1 tablespoon Sesame (Gingelly) Oil

Salt , to taste

Salt , to taste

How to make Thandu Keerai Puli Kuzhambu Recipe - Amaranth Greens in Tangy Curry

To begin making Thandu Keerai Puli Kuzhambu Recipe, soak tamarind in hot water, squeeze the pulp out and keep aside. You will have approximately 1-1/2 cups of tamarind water.

Heat sesame oil in a heavy bottomed pan, add the mustard seeds, and let it crackle.

Add the asafoetida, curry leaves and let it splutter.

Add the whole garlic cloves, chopped onions and saute until the garlic turns slightly golden and onions become soft.

Once the onions become soft, add chopped tomato and cook until it turns soft and mushy.

Next add the chopped thandu keerai or amaranth leaves and saute until the greens become soft.

After the Thandu Keerai/ Amaranth leaves turn soft, add the tamarind pulp, sambar powder, fenugreek powder and season with salt, mix well and let it simmer for 10 minutes on low heat. Add additional water if required to adjust the consistency of the kuzhambu.

Simmer and cook until the Thandu Keerai Puli Kuzhambu gets a little thicker. Once the Kuzhambu thickens, turn off the heat and serve hot.

Serve Thandu Keerai Puli Kuzhambu along with Steamed Rice, Kathirikai Kootu, Carrot and Beans Poriyal Recipe and Curd for a weeknight dinner.

Poondu Milagu Kuzhambu Recipe - Tamilnadu Style Garlic and Black Pepper Curry

A spicy and tangy kuzhambu prepared with the goodness of garlic and pepper, a perfect accompaniment for hot steamed rice and drizzle of sesame oil makes for a perfect midday lunch or dinner.

Poondu Milagu Kuzhambu is a traditional tamarind based curry prepared using garlic cloves and black pepper corns from the state of Tamil Nadu.

Since the Recipe contains garlic and peppercorns, it helps soothe a cold or cough. It is spicy and tangy, at the same time garlic adds a lot of flavour to the curry. It makes for a perfect accompaniment with hot steamed rice and a generous drizzle of sesame oil.

Serve Poondu Milagu Kuzhambu Recipe (Tamilnadu Style Tangy Garlic and Black Pepper Curry) along with Steamed Rice, Carrot and Chow Chow Kootu, Cabbage Poriyal and Vadams for a delicious Tamilnadu style weekend lunch.

Prep Time	:	10 Mins
Cooks Time	:	20 Mins
Total Time	:	30 Mins
Cuisine	:	Tamil Nadu
Serving	:	4 Servings

Equipments Used: Hard Anodised Kadai (Wok)

Ingredients

1/2 cup Garlic

1/2 teaspoon Turmeric powder (Haldi)

2 teaspoons Jaggery

1 teaspoon Mustard seeds (Rai/ Kadugu)

30 grams Tamarind

1/2 teaspoon Methi Seeds (Fenugreek Seeds)

1 sprig Curry leaves , washed

1 tablespoon Sesame (Gingelly) Oil

Ingredients to roast and grind

1/2 cup Garlic

1/2 cup Pearl onions (Sambar Onions) , peeled

1 Tomato , roughly chopped

3 teaspoons Whole Black Peppercorns

1 teaspoon Cumin seeds (Jeera)

2 Dry Red Chilli

2 sprig Curry leaves , washed

1 teaspoon Sesame (Gingelly) Oil

How to make Poondu Milagu Kuzhambu Recipe - Tamilnadu Style Garlic and Black Pepper Curry

To begin making Poondu Milagu Kuzhambu Recipe, soak the tamarind in warm water, extract the pulp and keep aside.

Heat oil in a heavy bottomed pan and roast the - garlic cloves, sambar onions, tomato, black peppercorns, cumin seeds, dried red chillies, curry leaves, sesame oil.

Roast till the raw smell of the onion and garlic goes away. Take off the flame and keep aside to cool.

Now, heat the sesame oil in a wide pan, add the mustard seeds, fenugreek seeds and let it crackle. Add the curry leaves and let it splutter.

Add in the garlic cloves and saute until it turns golden brown. Add the tamarind extract, turmeric powder and let it simmer for 5 minutes until the raw smell of the tamarind goes away.

Now, add in the prepared ground mixture, season with salt and mix well. Let this curry simmer for 10-15 minutes, till everything comes together and the oil separates out.

Now, add in the jaggery powder mix well and simmer for another 5 minutes. Serve hot.

Serve Poondu Milagu Kuzhambu Recipe (Tamilnadu Style Tangy Garlic and Black Pepper Curry) along with Steamed Rice, Carrot and Chow Chow Kootu, Cabbage Poriyal and Vadams for a delicious Tamilnadu style weekend lunch.

Brinjal Mor Kuzhambu Recipe

Brinjal Mor Kuzhambu Recipe is a delicious South Indian curry made with brinjals, and the addition of red chillies and tamarind that bring in a distinct flavor variation from the regular Mor Kuzhambu. Served best with some steamed rice for a comforting weekday lunch.

Brinjal Mor Kuzhambu Recipe, a variation to the regular Mor Kuzhambu. This one uses brinjals, in the curd based curry, with a tadka of mustard seeds, curry leaves and asafoetida that lend a lovely flavour to the dish.

You can replace the brinjals with any other veggies or your choice.

Serve the Brinjal Mor Kuzhambu Recipe along with steamed rice, Beetroot Poriyal Recipe or a Chow Chow Thoran (Poriyal) Recipe to make it a complete meal.

Prep Time   :   10 Mins

Cooks Time   :   45 Mins

Total Time	:	55 Mins
Cuisine	:	Tamil Nadu
Serving	:	4 Servings

Equipments Used: Hard Anodised Kadai (Wok)

Ingredients

3 Brinjal (Baingan / Eggplant) , cubed

1 cup Tamarind Water

1 teaspoon Turmeric powder (Haldi)

Salt , to taste

For the Curry

2 teaspoons Chana dal (Bengal Gram Dal)

2 teaspoons Arhar dal (Split Toor Dal)

2 teaspoons Rice

2 cup Curd (Dahi / Yogurt)

2 tablespoon Fresh coconut , pieces (adjust quantity according to taste)

For seasoning

2 teaspoons Oil

1 teaspoon Mustard seeds (Rai/ Kadugu)

1 teaspoon Black Urad Dal (Split)

3/4 teaspoons Methi Seeds (Fenugreek Seeds)

8-10 Curry leaves

5 Dry Red Chillies

1 pinch Asafoetida (hing)

How to make Brinjal Mor Kuzhambu Recipe

To begin making the Brinjal Mor Kuzhambu Recipe, soak the dals - chana dal, toor and rice in lukewarm water and rest it for at least 30 minutes.

Once done, grind the dals and rice with little water to a smooth paste and add coconut and curd and grind it again in the same mixer to a smooth paste and keep it aside.

Heat a kadai with oil, add chopped brinjal, sprinkle with salt and turmeric and cook till it becomes soft.

Pour in the tamarind water and allow it to cook for at least 15 minutes until the brinjal becomes quite mushy.

Mix in the curd and the freshly ground dal-rice paste into the kadai and stir well, sprinkle salt and pour in some more water to adjust the consistency.

Allow it to boil for at least 10 minutes until the raw smell of the rice and dal goes away. Switch off the heat and keep it aside.

Heat a tempering pan with oil, add mustard seeds , urad dal and fenugreek seeds and allow it to sizzle.

Add curry leaves and dry red chillies and allow it to crackle for a few seconds.

Sprinkle a pinch of hing at the end and pour this over the mor kuzhambu and serve hot.

Serve the Brinjal Mor Kuzhambu Recipe along with steamed rice, Beetroot Poriyal Recipe or a Chow Chow Thoran (Poriyal) Recipe to make it a complete meal.

Kongunadu Style Kalan kuzhambu Recipe - Mushroom Curry

Kongunadu Style Kalan kuzhambu Recipe is a lip smacking mushroom curry made South Indian style. Serve this with parottas for a lovely Sunday brunch.

Kongunadu Style Kalan kuzhambu Recipe is famous from the Coimbatore region of Tamil Nadu. Kongunadu is a part of Tamil Nadu Cuisine that majorly covers the western part of the state.

The mushroom kalan is prepared with ground spice and simmered to create a spicy broth. That way the mushroom can develop a lot of flavor and it is eaten along with parotta by the side.

Serve the Kongunadu Style Kalan kuzhambu Recipe along with parotta and Moong Sprouts Usal Recipe (Indian Salad Chaat).

Prep Time   :   10 Mins

Cooks Time   :   30 Mins

Total Time   :   40 Mins

Cuisine   :   Kongunadu

Serving   :   4 Servings

Equipments Used: Preethi Blue Leaf Mixer Grinder, Saucepan With Handle (Tea/Sauces)

Ingredients

500 grams Button mushrooms , quartered

1 Onion , chopped

1 Green Chilli , slit

1 sprig Curry leaves

1 teaspoon Mustard seeds (Rai/ Kadugu)

Salt , to taste

Oil

To Grind

2 tablespoon Coriander (Dhania) Seeds

3 Dry Red Chilli

1 inch Cinnamon Stick (Dalchini)

2 Cloves (Laung)

1 teaspoon Cumin seeds (Jeera)

1 teaspoon Fennel seeds (Saunf)

1 teaspoon Whole Black Peppercorns

1 Onion , chopped

4 cloves Garlic

1 inch Ginger

4 tablespoon Fresh coconut , grated

2 tablespoons Garam masala powder

How to make Kongunadu Style Kalan kuzhambu Recipe - Mushroom Curry

To begin making the Kongunadu Style Kalan kuzhambu Recipe, we will heat a skillet with oil, add cloves, cinnamon stick, peppercorns, fennel seeds and cumin seeds.

Allow it to sizzle for a few seconds. Add ginger and garlic and saute till they soften.

Add chopped onions and saute till they turn translucent and add grated coconut and saute till they turn light brown.

Add garam masala and mix well, cook for another 10 minutes and switch off the heat.

Rest for a few seconds and grind it along with water to a smooth paste.

Heat a kadai with oil, add mustard seeds and allow it to splutter for a few seconds, add curry leaves and allow it to crackle.

Add onions and saute till they turn translucent. Add in chopped green chillies and mushroom and toss well till the mushroom has cooked.

You can add the freshly ground paste now and mix well, check for salt and add 1 cup of water and cook for around 10 minutes until it comes to a rolling boil, turn off the flame, transfer into a serving bowl and serve hot.

Serve the Kongunadu Style Kalan kuzhambu Recipe along with parotta and Moong Sprouts Usal Recipe (Indian Salad Chaat).

Paruppu Urundai Mor Kuzhambu Recipe(Lentil Balls in Yogurt Curry)

A spicy toor dal ball that is soaked in a turmeric flavoured yogurt curry and tempered with mustard seeds and curry leaves.

Paruppu Urundai Mor Kuzhambu Recipe(Lentil Balls in Yogurt Curry) is a comforting yogurt based curry that you must try for your lunch meal. It consists of a spicy lentil mixture that is shaped into medium sized balls and then steamed. These steamed lentil balls are then cooked in a simple buttermilk and coconut curry. The curry has all the nutrients needed for your body. It is best served over hot steamed rice with a dollop of ghee.

Serve the Paruppu Urundai Mor Kuzhambu along with steamed rice, dollop of ghee and a poriyal by the side to finish lunch.

Prep Time   :   10 Mins

Cooks Time   :   30 Mins

Total Time   :   40 Mins

Cuisine   :   Tamil Nadu

Serving   :   4 Servings

Equipments Used: Preethi Blue Leaf Mixer Grinder, Stainless Steel 2 Tier Steamer, Hard Anodised Kadai (Wok)

Ingredients

For the Urundai

1/2 cup Arhar dal (Split Toor Dal)

2 Dry Red Chilli

1 pinch Asafoetida (hing)

4 cloves Garlic

1 sprig Curry leaves , chopped

1 sprig Coriander (Dhania) Leaves , chopped

1/4 teaspoon Turmeric powder (Haldi)

Salt , to taste

Oil

For the Curry

1 cup Buttermilk

2 tablespoon Fresh coconut , grated

1 Green Chilli

1 teaspoon Cumin seeds (Jeera)

1 teaspoon Rice flour

1/2 teaspoon Turmeric powder (Haldi)

Salt , to taste

For tempering

1 teaspoon Mustard seeds (Rai/ Kadugu)

1 sprig Curry leaves

1 Dry Red Chilli

How to make Paruppu Urundai Mor Kuzhambu Recipe(Lentil Balls in Yogurt Curry)

To begin making the Paruppu Urundai Mor Kuzhambu Recipe, we will first pressure cook the toor dal with water, turmeric powder and salt in a pressure cooker for about 2 whistles.

Once the pressure is released naturally, you can transfer the cooked toor dal into a mixing jar along with garlic, hing, dry red chillies and grind it into a smooth paste.

Heat a flat skillet with oil, add chopped curry leaves and allow it to splutter. Add ground dal mixture and mix till it all comes together.

At the end add chopped coriander leaves and mix well, switch off the flame and keep it aside to cool down.

Once it cools down, start shaping them into medium sized balls. You can keep a vegetable or Idli steamer on with water over the stove.

Once the steamer is heated up, place the balls inside the steamer and steam them for about 15 minutes till it firms up.

Meanwhile, grind coconut, green chilli, rice flour and cumin seeds in a mixer to a smooth paste by adding water.

Heat a sauce pan and mix buttermilk and ground coconut paste together, add turmeric powder, salt and bring it to a boil.

Slowly add the steamed lentil balls into the curry and boil on simmer for about 2 minutes. Switch off the heat and keep things ready for tempering.

Heat a small tadka pan, add oil, once it is heated up add mustard seeds, allow it to crackle and add curry leaves and dry red chilli. Let it splutter for a few seconds and pour this tadka over the curry and serve.

Serve the Paruppu Urundai Mor Kuzhambu along with steamed rice, dollop of ghee and a poriyal by the side to finish lunch.

Palakottai Kuzhambu Recipe-Kongunad Style Jackfruit Seeds Curry

Palakottai Kuzhambu Recipe is essentially Jackfruit seeds cooked in an aromatic base, Palakottai Kuzhambu Recipe is packed with flavours and is a must try recipe. Instead of discarding the seeds, this lovely curry can be made with it.

Palakottai Kuzhambu Recipe is Kongunad Style Jackfruit Seeds Curry. There are many variations in making this palakottai Kuzhambu.I have prepared palakottai in a coconut based puli Kuzhambu.

This is a common kuzhambu recipe that is popular in jackfruit growing areas of Tamil Nadu, and all of South India. With little modifications in the recipe, the jackfruit seeds are widely used as food in many parts of India.

Did you know: The Jackfruit seeds/palakottai are starchy and a good source of carbohydrates, besides it is also a source of healthy proteins, aiding in keeping a smooth functioning bowel, great for skin and hair as well!Serve Palakottai

Serve Palakottai Kuzhambu Recipe along with Raw Jackfruit Poriyal Recipe, Steamed Rice Recipe and Thayir Semiya Recipe for a hearty weekday lunch.

Prep Time   :   5 Mins

Cooks Time   :   20 Mins

Total Time   :   25 Mins

Cuisine   :   Tamil Nadu

Serving   :   4 Servings

Equipments Used: Hard Anodized Pressure Cooker

Ingredients

1 cup Jackfruit Seeds (Kathal)

1 cup Tamarind Water

8 cloves Garlic

1/2 teaspoon Mustard seeds (Rai/ Kadugu)

1/2 teaspoon Cumin seeds (Jeera)

8 Curry leaves

1/4 teaspoon Turmeric powder (Haldi)

1/2 teaspoon Red Chilli powder

2 teaspoons Sambar Powder

1/4 teaspoon Asafoetida (hing)

Coriander (Dhania) Leaves , small bunch, for garnishing

Salt , to taste

2 teaspoons Oil

To be ground

1/2 cup Fresh coconut

10 Whole Black Peppercorns

2 Dry Red Chillies

To saute and grind

1 Onion , chopped

1 Tomato , chopped

1 teaspoon Coriander (Dhania) Seeds

1 teaspoon Oil

How to make Palakottai Kuzhambu Recipe-Kongunad Style Jackfruit Seeds Curry

To begin making Palakottai Kuzhambu Recipe, wash the jackfruits seeds thoroughly, make a slit on the outer layer and remove the outer white layer.

In a pressure cooker, add the Jackfruit seeds, add enough water to submerge the seeds,add a pinch of salt, and pressure cook it on a high heat for 3-4 whistles or till they are cooked al-dente. Allow the pressure to release naturally. Drain and reserve the jackfruit seed stock for later use.

Heat a kadai on medium flame, add oil once the oil is hot, add onions and saute until almost translucent, for about 2-3 minutes.

Now add chopped tomatoes , cover and cook until the tomatoes are mushy. Transfer the sauteed onion-tomatoes and allow them to cool.

Transfer the onion-tomato mixture into a mixer-jar, add coriander seeds and grind well along with some of the jackfruit stock. We need a smooth paste. Transfer to a bowl and set aside.

Yet again, in a mixer grinder, combine fresh grated coconut, red chillies and black pepper along with a little jackfruit seeds stock, and grind to a smooth paste. Keep aside.

Heat a pan with oil, on medium heat, add mustard seeds and cumin seeds and curry leaves. Once they splutter and sizzle, add in asafoetida and the crushed garlic cloves and saute till the garlic turn golden.

Once garlic turns to golden, add the ground onion tomato paste and saute well until it starts boiling.

Add the tamarind water to it and stir. Boil for 2-3 minutes and cook palakottai/jackfruit seeds. Mix well.

Add required salt, turmeric powder, chilli powder, sambar powder. Mix well and cook for 5 minutes in medium heat, such that the flavours seep into the jackfruit seeds.

Now add the ground coconut mixture and stir well. Cook on a low heat until it thickens. Taste and adjust seasoning and consistency of the Palakottai Kuzhambu to your liking. Turn off the flame.

Garnish with coriander leaves.

Serve Palakottai Kuzhambu Recipe along with Raw
Jackfruit Poriyal Recipe, Steamed Rice Recipe and
Thayir Semiya Recipe for a hearty weekday lunch.

Sorakkai Paruppu Kuzhambu Recipe - Tamil Nadu Style Lauki Curry

Sorakkai Paruppu Kuzhambu is a delicious and
super healthy South Indian curry where bottle
gourd is cooked with lentils to make a tangy curry.
Best served with steamed rice and a dollop of
ghee.

Sorakkai Paruppu Kuzhambu Recipe is a side dish
recipe to prepare that can be done in about 20
minutes and hence is a great recipe for a busy

weeknight dinner. Made with nutritious summer vegetable-bottle gourd, the curry is full of nutrients and is a coolant to the body as well.

Usually kuzhambu is a South Indian gravy that is made with tangy tamarind or cooked along with coconut and other spices like sambar powder. Here I have used a tamarind base for the recipe to be tangy and addition if dal/pappu makes it creamy and hearty.

Kuzhambu, in general- is a staple that is made in every Tamil household on a day-to-day basis.

Did you know: Bottle Gourd has 90% water in it. Bottle Gourd is recommended by Ayurveda for better digestion. Because of its water content, it's a boon for weight watchers. It can help in quenching extreme thirst in diabetic patients. Loaded with essential minerals and vitamins like calcium, magnesium, phosphorus, Vitamin A, C and folate, it's popular for combating high blood pressure and improving heart health.

Serve Sorakkai Paruppu Kuzhambu Recipe along with Steamed Rice, Carrot and Beans Poriyal Recipe, Phulka and Kathirikai Pitlai Recipe to make it a complete meal.

Prep Time   :   10 Mins

Cooks Time   :   15 Mins

Total Time   :   25 Mins

Cuisine   :   Tamil Nadu

Serving   :   6 Servings

Equipments Used: Hard Anodized Pressure
Cooker, Hard Anodised Frying Pan / Omelette Pan

Ingredients

1 cup Bottle gourd (lauki) , cut into medium sized
pieces

1 cup Yellow Moong Dal (Split) , washed and
soaked

1 teaspoon Ghee

1/2 teaspoon Mustard seeds (Rai/ Kadugu)

1/2 teaspoon Cumin seeds (Jeera)

1 sprig Curry leaves , torn

2 Dry Red Chillies , broken

10 Pearl onions (Sambar Onions) , quartered

1 Tomato , finely chopped

1/2 cup Tamarind Water

1/4 teaspoon Turmeric powder (Haldi)

1 tablespoon Sambar Powder

Salt

6 sprig Coriander (Dhania) Leaves , finely chopped

How to make Sorakkai Paruppu Kuzhambu Recipe - Tamil Nadu Style Lauki Curry

To begin making Sorakkai Paruppu Kuzhambu Recipe, into the pressure cooker combine the bottle gourd, yellow moong dal, tomatoes, salt, turmeric powder and half a cup of water.

Pressure cook this for two whistles and turn off the heat. Allow the cooker to release the pressure naturally. Keep aside.

Heat ghee over medium heat in a heavy bottom pan; add the mustard seeds and cumin seeds, and allow them to crackle.

Next add the curry leaves, dry red chillies and onions and saute for about a minute or until the onions turn transparent and golden brown.

Once the onions have turned golden, add the tamarind water, sambar powder and allow it to come to a brisk boil for 3 to 4 minutes till the raw taste from the tamarind goes away.

Finally add in the bottle-gourd dal mixture and bring the Sorakkai Paruppu Kuzhambu to a brisk boil. Once done, turn check the salt and adjust to taste accordingly.

Stir in chopped coriander leaves to the Sorakkai Paruppu Kuzhambu and serve hot.

Serve hot Sorakkai Paruppu Kuzhambu Recipe along with Steamed Rice, Carrot and Beans Poriyal Recipe, Phulka and Kathirikai Pitlai Recipe to make it a complete meal.

Vendakkai-Vazhakkai Mor Kuzhambu Recipe (Tamil Nadu Style Lady's Finger & Raw Banana Curry)

Delicious but cooling veggies in buttermilk gravy

Vendakkai-Vazhakkai Mor Kuzhambu Recipe is a Tamil Nadu Style Lady's Finger & Raw Banana Curry cooked in buttermilk. This is a popular side dish along with steamed rice. In Tamil Nadu, this Mor kuzhambu is prepared with mixed vegetables or a single vegetable, is tangy and flavourful if made with mixed vegetables.

Serve Vendakkai-Vazhakkai Mor Kuzhambu Recipe (Tamil Nadu Style Lady's Finger & Raw Banana Curry) along with steamed rice and Phulka sided with Urulaikizhangu Podi (Spicy Potato Crumble from Tamil Nadu) Recipe and Tamil Nadu Style Muttaikose Pattani Poriyal Recipe.

Prep Time	:	10 Mins
Cooks Time	:	20 Mins
Total Time	:	30 Mins
Cuisine	:	Tamil Nadu
Serving	:	4 Servings

Equipments Used: Preethi Blue Leaf Mixer Grinder, Saucepan With Handle (Tea/Sauces), Tadka Pan (Seasoning Pan)

Ingredients

2 cups Buttermilk

1 cup Bhindi (Lady Finger/Okra) , chopped

1 cup Raw Banana

1/4 teaspoon Turmeric powder (Haldi)

To be ground

1 tablespoon Broken Raw Rice

1 tablespoon Arhar dal (Split Toor Dal)

2 tablespoons Coriander (Dhania) Seeds

1/2 inch Ginger , grated

2 Green Chillies , slit

1/4 cup Fresh coconut

For tempering

1 tablespoon Mustard seeds (Rai/ Kadugu)

2 Dry Red Chillies , broken

1/2 teaspoon Asafoetida (hing)

1 sprig Curry leaves

2 teaspoons Oil

How to make Vendakkai-Vazhakkai Mor Kuzhambu Recipe (Tamil Nadu Style Lady's Finger & Raw Banana Curry)

To begin making Vendakkai-Vazhakkai Mor Kuzhambu Recipe (Tamil Nadu Style Lady's Finger & Raw Banana Curry), In a kadai, stir fry the ladies finger.

Add the raw bananas/vazhakkai once the vendakkai is half done and stir well till the sliminess of the vendakkai disappears. Make sure you stir lightly just to avoid burning and avoid them getting any mushy or breaking. Keep them aside.

Also meanwhile in a mixer grinder, grind all the ingredients mentioned under "to be ground". Once the mixture is crumbly, add water and grind further till it becomes paste-like.

In a saucepan, add a little oil. When the oil is heated, add the ground mixture, turmeric powder, cover and cook it with a little water till the rice and dal are cooked, on a medium heat. Mine took about five minutes. (you can skip adding oil here, since however the dal and rice needs to be cooked in water).

Add the buttermilk, salt and whisk it till it is properly mixed.

Add the fried vendakkai and vazhakkai (bhindi and raw bananas). Continue medium heat.

Meanwhile in a tadka pan, add oil. To this, add mustard seeds and allow to crackle. Once the mustard crackles, add asafoetida, curry leaves and dried red chillies, stir and switch off heat.

When the butter milk starts to froth up from the edges of the pan, add the tempering and turn off the flame. Do not boil after adding the butter milk.

Give Mor kuzhambu a nice mix and cover for 5 minutes before serving.

Serve Vendakkai-Vazhakkai Mor Kuzhambu Recipe (Tamil Nadu Style Lady's Finger & Raw Banana Curry) along with steamed rice and Phulka sided with Urulaikizhangu Podi (Spicy Potato Crumble from Tamil Nadu) Recipe and Tamil Nadu Style Muttaikose Pattani Poriyal Recipe.

Note:

Any vegetables of your choice can be added

Pachai Sundakkai Puli Kuzhambu Recipe (Turkey Berry Tamarind Based Gravy)

Tangy and yummy crushed Turkey berries cooked with coconut and tamarind to make kuzhambu

Sundakkai puli kuzhambu is a delicious south Indian chettinad style kuzhambu prepared with fresh sundakkai. The sundakkai is crushed before preparing to reduce the bitterness. It is coconut based puli kuzhambu that goes well with rice and dosa. You can also prepare vathal kuzhambu with these berries.

Serve Pachai Sundakkai Puli Kuzhambu Recipe (Turkey Berry Tamarind Based Gravy) with Steamed Rice, Elai Vadam Recipe, Healthy Maravalli Kizhangu Bonda Recipe and Cabbage Thoran (Poriyal) Recipe to make it a complete meal.

Prep Time	:	10 Mins
Cooks Time	:	30 Mins
Total Time	:	40 Mins
Cuisine	:	South Indian
Serving	:	5 Servings

Equipments Used: Saucepan With Handle (Tea/Sauces), Hard Anodised Kadai (Wok)

Ingredients

1 cup Sundakkai (Turkey Berries)

1 Onion , chopped

1 Tomato , chopped

6 cloves Garlic

4 Dry Red Chillies

1 cup Tamarind Water

1/4 teaspoon Turmeric powder (Haldi)

2 teaspoon Sambar Powder

1/2 teaspoon Mustard seeds (Rai/ Kadugu)

1/2 teaspoon Cumin seeds (Jeera)

1 sprig Curry leaves

Salt

3 teaspoon Oil

1 teaspoon Sugar , (optional)

To grind:

1/2 cup Fresh coconut

1 teaspoon Coriander (Dhania) Seeds

1 teaspoon Fennel seeds (Saunf)

How to make Pachai Sundakkai Puli Kuzhambu Recipe (Turkey Berry Tamarind Based Gravy)

To begin making Pachai Sundakkai Puli Kuzhambu Recipe (Turkey Berry Tamarind Based Gravy), wash the sundakkai well and crush them using mortar and pestle. Crushing is important to remove bitterness from the berry.

Take coconut, Fennel seeds, Coriander seeds in a blender. Add a little water and grind into a smooth paste. Keep aside.

Heat oil in a Kadai, add mustard seeds and cumin seeds once the oil is hot. Once they splutter, add curry leaves and red chilli and saute for a few seconds.

Add sliced onions now and saute well until the onions turn translucent.

Once the onions are translucent, add the crushed garlic and saute until raw smell goes, for about a few seconds.

Add chopped tomatoes and cook until they turn mushy. Add the crushed sundakkai and saute for a minute.

Now add the tamarind juice and mix well. Add turmeric powder, sambar powder and required salt.

Stir and cook on a medium heat until sundakkai gets cooked well and everything seems combined.

Add the ground coconut paste and mix well. Reduce the flame to low and cook for a few minutes until the kuzhambu thickens.

Add sugar and mix. Garnish with coriander leaves and switch off heat.

Serve Pachai Sundakkai Puli Kuzhambu Recipe (Turkey Berry Tamarind Based Gravy) with Steamed Rice, Elai Vadam Recipe, Healthy Maravalli Kizhangu Bonda Recipe and Cabbage Thoran (Poriyal) Recipe to make it a complete meal.

Appalam Vatha Kuzhambu Recipe - Papad In Tamarind Gravy

A tangy, spicy and delicious Appalam Vatha Kuzhambu is an absolute must try. The tamarind curry gets its delicious taste and flavours from the sesame oil, along with the tadka and the homemade sambar powder. Serve it along with Paruppu Usili and hot steamed rice for lunch or dinner.

The Appalam Vatha Kuzhambu is a classic south indian preparation which has delicate flavours from the papad and the onions along with sambar powder simmered to make a spicy and tangy curry. You can use any papad of your choice, however the ulundu appalam or the urad dal papad tastes best in this vathal kuzhambu.

Serve the Appalam Vatha Kuzhambu along with hot Steamed Rice, Bean Paruppu Usili and Elai Vadam for a simple and delicious weekend lunch.

Prep Time	:	5 Mins
Cooks Time	:	20 Mins
Total Time	:	25 Mins
Cuisine	:	South Indian
Serving	:	3 Servings

Equipments Used: Hard Anodised Kadai (Wok)

Ingredients

1 tablespoon Gingelly oil

1/4 teaspoon Mustard seeds (Rai/ Kadugu)

1/4 teaspoon Methi Seeds (Fenugreek Seeds)

Asafoetida (hing) , a pinch

3 Dry Red Chillies

1/2 cup Pearl onions (Sambar Onions) , halved

1 sprig Curry leaves

3 Urad dal papad , broken in to quarters

1 cup Tamarind Water

1 teaspoon Sambar Powder

1 tablespoon Jaggery

1/4 teaspoon Turmeric powder (Haldi)

3 cups Water

Salt , as needed

How to make Appalam Vatha Kuzhambu Recipe - Papad In Tamarind Gravy

To begin making the Appalam Vatha Kuzhambu recipe, prepare all the ingredients and keep them ready.

Heat oil in a preheated pan over medium heat. Add mustard seeds, fenugreek seeds, curry leaves and dried red chilies. Allow it to crackle.

Add the onions and saute until the onions have softened and lightly golden.

Once the onions have softened, add the tamarind water, turmeric powder, sambar powder, jaggery and appalam.

Add 3 cups of water, salt to taste and simmer the appalam vatha kuzhambu, until the kuzhambu has thickened and the appalam has soaked and cooked through as well.

The Appalam Vatha Kuzhambu will have a gravy-like consistency with the starch from the appalam giving it this texture. Adjust the consistency of the kuzhambu by adding water and also check the salt and spices and adjust to taste accordingly

Serve the Appalam Vatha Kuzhambu along with hot Steamed Rice, Bean Paruppu Usili and Elai Vadam for a simple and delicious weekend lunch.

Chettinad Style Kara Kuzhambu Recipe with Potato and Brinjal

Chettinad Style Kara Kuzhambu Recipe with Potato and Brinjal is a robust Chettinad style kuzhambu with added goodness of potatoes and brinjals. Serve best with steamed rice for a satisfying weekday meal.

Chettinad Style Kara Kuzhambu Recipe with Potato and Brinjal is a finger licking good recipe made the Chettinad way.

The pearl onions in the kuzhambu along with the freshly ground spice masala and sambar powder give it a rich taste. Add potatoes and brinjal, add nutrition and completely elevate the kara kuzhambu.

Serve Chettinad Style Kara Kuzhambu Recipe with Potato and Brinjal along with Steamed Rice,

Beetroot Thoran and Elai Vadam for a weekday meal.

Prep Time	:	15 Mins
Cooks Time	:	60 Mins
Total Time	:	75 Mins
Cuisine	:	South Indian
Serving	:	4 Servings

Equipments Used: Preethi Blue Leaf Mixer Grinder, Hard Anodised Kadai (Wok)

Ingredients

For ground masala

1/4 teaspoon Methi Seeds (Fenugreek Seeds)

2 teaspoons Coriander (Dhania) Seeds

1 teaspoon Fennel seeds (Saunf)

2 Dry Red Chillies

1/4 cup Fresh coconut , grated

For the Kuzhambu

1/2 cup Pearl onions (Sambar Onions) , quartered

5 cloves Garlic , finely chopped

2 Tomatoes , finely chopped

2 Potatoes (Aloo) , cut into medium sized pieces

2 Brinjal (Baingan / Eggplant) , cut into wedges

1 tablespoon Jaggery

1 cup Tamarind Water

1 teaspoon Sambar Powder

For seasoning

1 teaspoon Gingelly oil

1/2 teaspoon Mustard seeds (Rai/ Kadugu)

2 sprig Curry leaves

How to make Chettinad Style Kara Kuzhambu Recipe with Potato and Brinjal

To begin making the Chettinad Style Kara Kuzhambu Recipe, we will first make the masala.

Heat a small pan on medium heat; add fenugreek seeds, coriander seeds, fennel seeds, red chillies. Roast these spices until the aroma wafts in the air. Stir in the freshly grated coconut and roast for another 2 to 3 minutes.

Turn off the heat and allow the spices to cool. Transfer the spices into a mixer jar, add 1/2 cup warm water and grind to make a smooth paste.

To cook the kara kuzhambu, heat oil in a pressure cooker over medium heat; add the onion, garlic and saute for a few minutes until the onion softens. Add the chopped tomatoes and saute until the tomatoes are mushy.

Stir in the potatoes, brinjal, jaggery, tamarind water, sambar powder and salt. Pressure cook for 3 to whistles and turn off the heat and allow the pressure to release naturally.

In the meantime, make the seasoning; heat oil in a tadka pan; add the mustard seeds and curry leaves and allow it to crackle. Turn off the heat and keep aside.

Once the pressure releases, stir in the coconut mixture, the seasoning mixture and give the Chetinnad Kara Kuzhambu a brisk boil for 3 to 4 minutes. Check the salt and adjust according to taste.

Serve hot Chettinad Style Potato Kara Kuzhambu along with Steamed Rice, Beetroot Thoran and Elai Vadam for a weekday meal.

Tamil Nadu Style Karamani Murungakkai Kuzhambu Recipe-Black eyed Beans & Drumstick Curry

Roasted onion gravy simmered with Black eyed beans and drumstick, flavoured with chettinad spices like cinnamon sticks, cardamom and peppercorns. The black eyed beans are rich in Vitamin A whereas drumstick pods help in building stronger bones and improves digestion and protects against infection. You can serve it along with some hot steamed rice and vendakkai poriyal by the side.

Tamil Nadu Style Karamani Murungakkai Kuzhambu Recipe-Black eyed Beans and Drumstick Curry is a recipe made without coconut as the base. The onions and fennel seeds are roasted well till it becomes golden brown and then ground into a smooth creamy paste which is then simmered with black eyed beans and drumstick.The black eyed beans is a rich source of vitamin A and dietary fibers.

Did you know ? Drumstick pods help to build strong bones, it is very good for pregnant women also. Drumstick pods which are known as moringa in the local language are rich in calcium, Iron and vitamins. They also have properties such as purifying the blood, improves digestion and protects against infection.

Serve the Tamil Nadu Style Karamani Murungakkai Kuzhambu Recipe can be serve along with Dry Fry Keema Balls (Spicy Chicken Keema Balls) Recipe ,Thakkali Rasam Recipe (South Indian Tomato Rasam) and rice to make it a meal.

Prep Time	:	10 Mins
Cooks Time	:	35 Mins
Total Time	:	45 Mins
Cuisine	:	Tamil Nadu
Serving	:	4 Servings

Equipments Used: Preethi Blue Leaf Mixer Grinder, Hard Anodized Pressure Cooker, Hard Anodised Kadai (Wok)

Ingredients

1/2 cup Black Eyed Beans (Lobia) , soaked in water for 2 hours

1 Drumstick , cut into 2 inch stripes

1 cup Pearl onions (Sambar Onions)

4 cloves Garlic , crushed

1 Cinnamon Stick (Dalchini)

2 Cloves (Laung)

1 Cardamom (Elaichi) Pods/Seeds

1 teaspoon Whole Black Peppercorns , crushed

1 teaspoon Coriander Powder (Dhania)

1 teaspoon Red Chilli powder

Salt , to taste

Oil , for cooking

1 Onions , chopped

1 teaspoon Fennel seeds (Saunf)

2 Dry Red Chilli

How to make Tamil Nadu Style Karamani Murungakkai Kuzhambu Recipe- Black eyed Beans & Drumstick Curry

We begin making the Tamil Nadu Style Karamani Murungakkai Kuzhambu Recipe by pressure cooking the karamani (Black eyed beans) and drumstick in the pressure cooker with 1/4 cup water and salt for about 2 whistles.

Release the pressure naturally and keep it aside. Heat a skillet with oil and fry the chopped onions, fennel seeds and dry red chilli till it is golden brown and cool it down. Grind it into a smooth paste.

Heat a kadai, with oil and fry the whole spices (cardamom, cloves, cinnamon, whole peppercorns) for a few seconds till the aroma comes out. Then add in the pearl onions and garlic, sauté till it is translucent.

Add in the ground paste along with all the spice powders (coriander powder & red chilli powder). Check for salt and you can add 1 cup water and stir well. Add in the cooked beans and drumstick. Stir well and simmer the Karamani Murungakkai Kuzhambu for at least 15 minutes and serve.

Serve the Tamil Nadu Style Karamani Murungakkai Kuzhambu Recipe can be served along with Dry Fry Keema Balls (Spicy Chicken Keema Balls) Recipe ,Thakkali Rasam Recipe (South Indian Tomato Rasam) and rice to make it a meal.

Iyengar Vendakkai Mor kuzhambu Recipe

You will simply love this Iyengar Style Vendakkai Mor kuzhambu Recipe which has crispy okra that is cooked in a thick , spicy yogurt based curry. Perfect to be served along with hot steamed rice and a poriyal.

Iyengar Style Vendakkai Mor Kuzhambu Recipe is a variant to the regular Poosanikai Mor Kuzhambu .This type of preparation is something very commonly seen in many Iyengars (a sect of Tambrahms Community) households. In other words it is also called as a south Indian version of "Bhindi Kadhi ". In the south Indian version of mor kuzhambu, It does not require Garam masala or garlic. The specialty in our cuisine is without these ingredients we can prepare an equally flavorful dish. Vendakkai Mor kuzhambu , is typically crispy okra that is cooked in a thick , spicy yogurt based sauce.

Serve the Iyengar Style Vendakkai Mor kuzhambu with hot steaming Rice and Raw Banana Thoran as a side dish to enjoy your perfect meal.)

Prep Time	:	30 Mins
Cooks Time	:	15 Mins
Total Time	:	45 Mins
Cuisine	:	Tamil Nadu
Serving	:	4 Servings

Equipments Used: Preethi Blue Leaf Mixer Grinder, Saucepan With Handle (Tea/Sauces)

Ingredients

For the Okra fry

8 Bhindi (Lady Finger/Okra)

2 tablespoons Coconut Oil

1 tablespoon Ghee

Salt , to taste

For roasting and grinding

3 tablespoons Arhar dal (Split Toor Dal)

1 pinch Turmeric powder (Haldi)

2 teaspoon Methi Seeds (Fenugreek Seeds)

2 teaspoon Cumin seeds (Jeera)

2 tablespoons Fresh coconut

1/2 inch Ginger , chopped

2 Green Chillies , chopped

2 Dry Red Chillies

2 sprig Coriander (Dhania) Leaves , chopped

Water , as required

For the Yogurt gravy

250 ml Curd (Dahi / Yogurt)

100 ml Water

Salt , to taste

For Tempering

1 teaspoon Ghee

1 teaspoon Mustard seeds (Rai/ Kadugu)

1 pinch Asafoetida (hing)

3 Dry Red Chillies

How to make Iyengar Vendakkai Mor kuzhambu Recipe

We begin Making the Iyengar Style Vendakkai Mor kuzhambu Recipe by soaking the toor dal in 1/2 cup lukewarm water and adding a little turmeric powder and leaving it in a blender jar for about 30 minutes.

Meanwhile, take a wok , on medium heat , add oil and saute fenugreek seeds, green chillies ,ginger pieces and dry red chillies until aromatic .

Transfer this roasted mixture to the soaking toor dal and add coconut scrapings , coriander leaves and cumin seed . Grind this to a fine paste.

In the same wok , on medium heat , add 2 tablespoons of coconut oil and 1 tablespoon of ghee , and fry the chopped okra until crispy. You can sprinkle little salt over it and saute until the outer skin of the okra turns light brown.

In a medium sized vessel , add the ground paste and whisk in 250 ml of sour curd and 100 ml of water without any lumps. Keep this on medium heat and stir continuously , do not leave this on heat without stirring , it will burn at the bottom and give a smoky taste.

Care must be taken. As you stir this , it will start boiling and the liquid will start to thicken. The liquid will froth in the sides.Now add the fried okra to this and stir. Switch off the heat and keep it aside.

Take a tempering pan or use the same wok that you used to fry the grinding ingredients and the okra , add a teaspoon of ghee, temper mustard seeds , asafoetida and break the dry red chillies and then add it. Saute this and add it to the Mor kuzhambu.

Serve the Iyengar Style Vendakkai Mor kuzhambu with hot steaming Rice and Raw Banana Thoran as a side dish to enjoy your perfect meal.

Murungakkai Mor Kuzhambu Recipe-Drumstick Buttermilk Curry

Drumstick dunked into the spicy and light buttermilk gravy that can be made for your lazy Sunday meal with a bowl of steamed rice by the side. Drumsticks are known to be beneficial to human beings in many ways. It is a rich source of protein and Vitamin C.

Murungakkai Mor Kuzhambu Recipe-Drumstick Buttermilk Curry is an easy way to make a curry by using curd as a base. The drumsticks are dunked into the spicy and light buttermilk gravy and can be made quickly on a busy day.

Did you know ? Drumstick pods help to build strong bones, it is very good for pregnant women also. Drumstick pods which are known as moringa in the local language are rich in calcium, Iron and vitamins. They also have properties such as purifying the blood, improves digestion and protects against infection.Drumsticks are known to be beneficial to human beings in many ways. It is a rich source of protein and Vitamin C.

Serve the Murungakkai Mor Kuzhambu Recipe-Drumstick Buttermilk Curry along with Cheppankizhangu Roast and steamed rice to enjoy your afternoon Lunch.

Prep Time	:	10 Mins
Cooks Time	:	20 Mins
Total Time	:	30 Mins
Cuisine	:	Tamil Nadu
Serving	:	4 Servings

Equipments Used: Preethi Blue Leaf Mixer Grinder, Hard Anodized Pressure Cooker, Hard Anodised Kadai (Wok), Tadka Pan (Seasoning Pan)

Ingredients

1 Drumstick , cut into 1 inch

1/2 cup Curd (Dahi / Yogurt)

1/2 teaspoon Turmeric powder (Haldi)

1/2 cup Fresh coconut , grated

1 teaspoon Rice , soaked in warm water

1 teaspoon Coriander (Dhania) Seeds , roasted

1 teaspoon Cumin seeds (Jeera)

2 Dry Red Chillies

Salt , to taste

To season

1 teaspoon Coconut Oil

1 teaspoon Mustard seeds (Rai/ Kadugu)

1 sprig Curry leaves , roughly torn

How to make Murungakkai Mor Kuzhambu Recipe-Drumstick Buttermilk Curry

To begin making the Murungakkai Mor Kuzhambu Recipe, first steam the drumstick in the pressure cooker, adding 2 tablespoons of water. Cook until you hear two whistles and turn off the heat. Release the pressure immediately so the green color remains and the drumsticks do not over cook, keep aside.

Grind the coconut, raw rice, cumin seeds, coriander seeds and red chillies into a smooth paste. Add a little warm water to help it grind well.

Add the yogurt, the coconut mixture and the cooked drumstick into a sauce pan and bring it to a brisk boil and turn off the heat.

For the seasoning, heat oil in a tadka pan over medium heat. Add the mustard seeds and allow it to crackle. Stir in the curry leaves and turn off the heat.

Pour the seasoning over the Murungakkai Mor Kuzhambu and serve.

Serve the Murungakkai Mor Kuzhambu Recipe along with Cheppankizhangu Roast and steamed rice to enjoy your afternoon Lunch.

kondai kadalai Vazhaithandu Puli Thengai Kuzhambu Recipe (Banana Stem Curry with Black Chickpeas Recipe)

kondai kadalai Vazhathandu Puli Thengai Kuzhambu Recipe (Banana Stem Curry with Black Chickpeas Recipe) is a healthy, whole hearted

Tamil Nadu style curry made with ground coconut and other spices and tossed in a tangy gravy.

Banana Stem is a good ingredient to be added to our day to day diet as it is diabetic friendly and also helps solve any gastric related problem.

Serve the kondai kadalai Vazhaithandu Puli Thengai Kuzhambu Recipe (Banana Stem Curry with Black Chickpeas Recipe) along with steam rice or Hot Phulka to enjoy your dinner meal.

Prep Time   :   500 Mins

Cooks Time   :   30 Mins

Total Time   :   530 Mins

Cuisine   :   Tamil Nadu

Serving   :   4 Servings

Equipments Used: Hard Anodized Pressure Cooker, Hard Anodised Kadai (Wok)

Ingredients

1 cup Kala Chana (Brown Chickpeas) , soaked in water overnight

250 grams Banana Stem , skin peeled and cut into small pieces

Salt , to taste

1 teaspoon Turmeric powder (Haldi)

To be ground to paste

1 teaspoon Methi Seeds (Fenugreek Seeds)

2 teaspoon White Urad Dal (Split)

3 Dry Red Chilli

1 tablespoon Coriander (Dhania) Seeds

1/2 cup Fresh coconut , grated

1 cup Tamarind Water

Seasoning

1/2 teaspoon Sesame (Gingelly) Oil

1/2 teaspoon Mustard seeds (Rai/ Kadugu)

2 sprig Curry leaves , roughly torn

How to make kondai kadalai Vazhaithandu Puli Thengai Kuzhambu Recipe (Banana Stem Curry with Black Chickpeas Recipe)

We begin making the kondai kadalai Vazhaithandu Puli Thengai Kuzhambu Recipe (Banana Stem Curry with Black Chickpeas Recipe) by pressure cooking the Kala chana with some water first in the pressure cooker for 4 whistles. Release the pressure naturally.

Then empty the black chickpea into a bowl, then in the same pressure cooker, add the banana stem with little water, salt and cook it for 1 whistle and rest.

Heat a heavy bottomed pan, add oil and crackle mustard seeds and curry leaves. Then add the ground paste and sauté for a few minutes, you can add little water.

Finally add the cooked banana stem and chickpeas, season it well and add some water to make it a little gravish.

Serve the kondai kadalai Vazhaithandu Puli Thengai Kuzhambu Recipe (Banana Stem Curry with Black Chickpeas Recipe) along with steam rice or Hot Phulka to enjoy your dinner meal.

Poricha Kuzhambu Recipe (Tamil Nadu Style Mixed Vegetables and Lentil Stew)

Poricha Kuzhambu is a traditional recipe from the Tirunelveli region of Tamil Nadu. It is a mixed vegetables and lentil stew, prepared using the mildly spiced coconut mix. It makes for a wonderful side dish with steamed rice. Since it uses mild spices, it is easy on the tummy as well.

Serve the Poricha Kuzhambu along with steamed rice, Manathakkali Kai Vathal Kuzhambu, Carrot and Beans Poriyal Recipe and potato roast for a full course Tamil Nadu style lunch menu on the weekend.

Prep Time	:	10 Mins
Cooks Time	:	20 Mins
Total Time	:	30 Mins
Cuisine	:	Tamil Nadu
Serving	:	4 Servings

Equipments Used: Hard Anodized Pressure Cooker, Tadka Pan (Seasoning Pan)

Ingredients

1/2 cup Arhar dal (Split Toor Dal) , cooked

1/2 cup Carrots (Gajjar) , finely chopped

1/2 cup Green peas (Matar)

1/2 cup Green beans (French Beans) , finely chopped

1/2 cup Cauliflower (gobi) , cut into small florets

2 tablespoons Fresh coconut , grated

1 teaspoon Cumin seeds (Jeera)

2 Dry Red Chilli

1 teaspoon Rice , soaked

1/2 teaspoon Turmeric powder (Haldi)

1 teaspoon Mustard seeds (Rai/ Kadugu)

1/2 teaspoon White Urad Dal (Split)

1 sprig Curry leaves

Salt , to taste

How to make Poricha Kuzhambu Recipe (Tamil Nadu Style Mixed Vegetables and Lentil Stew)

To begin making Poricha Kuzhambu, wash and soak the toor dal for 30 minutes and then pressure cook using a cooker for 3 whistles and keep aside.

Make a smooth paste of grated coconut, soaked raw rice, cumin seeds and red chillies using a hand blender and keep aside.

Now take a big wok, add all the vegetables, 1/2 glass of water, turmeric powder, salt and cook until the vegetables are well cooked in medium flame.

Add the cooked dal to the vegetables, water to your required consistency and bring it to a rolling boil.

Now, add the ground spice mix, season with salt and let it simmer for 10 minutes to thicken and switch off the flame.

Heat a small tadka pan on medium heat, add the mustard seeds and urad dal and let it crackle.

Add the curry leaves and let it splutter and pour this tadka over the Poricha Kuzhambu.

Serve the Poricha Kuzhambu along with steamed rice, Manathakkali Kai Vathal Kuzhambu, Carrot and Beans Poriyal Recipe and potato roast for a full course Tamil Nadu style lunch menu on the weekend.

kondai kadalai Puli Vengaya Kuzhambu Recipe (South Indian Style Spicy And Tangy Kala Chana)

The kondai kadalai Puli Vengaya Kuzhambu Recipe is a delicious spicy and tangy recipe from south india, where black chana also known as kala chana is cooked and simmered in a tamarind tomato curry that is spiced with sambar powder as a core ingredient. Kuzhambu are classic dishes from south india, that are most often served along with steamed rice, dosa, idli or even paratha.

Serve the kondai kadalai Puli Vengaya Kuzhambu along with Beetroot Poriyal and hot steamed rice for lunch or dinner.

Prep Time	:	10 Mins
Cooks Time	:	30 Mins
Total Time	:	40 Mins
Cuisine	:	Chettinad
Serving	:	4 Servings

Equipments Used: Hard Anodized Pressure Cooker

Ingredients

1 cup Kala Chana (Brown Chickpeas)

12 Pearl onions (Sambar Onions) , halved

1 tablespoon Sambar Powder

1 teaspoon Turmeric powder (Haldi)

1 teaspoon Jaggery

1 cup Tamarind Water

1/2 cup Homemade tomato puree

1/2 teaspoon Mustard seeds (Rai/ Kadugu)

1/4 teaspoon Methi Seeds (Fenugreek Seeds)

1 sprig Curry leaves , roughly torn

Salt , to taste

Sesame (Gingelly) Oil , for cooking

How to make kondai kadalai Puli Vengaya Kuzhambu Recipe (South Indian Style Spicy And Tangy Kala Chana)

To begin making the kondai kadalai Puli Vengaya Kuzhambu Recipe, first soak the kala chan (kondai kadalai) in water for at least 8 hours.

Cook the kondai kadalai with salt and water in the Pressure cooker for about 7 to 8 whistles. Turn the heat to low and simmer for another 15 minutes. Ensure that the kondai kadalai is cooked well. Once done, keep aside.

Heat oil in a pan, add the mustard seeds, fenugreek seeds and allow them to crackle. Add the onions, curry leaves and roast the onions until tender. Add the tamarind water, tomato puree, jaggery, sambar powder, turmeric powder, cooked kondai kadalai and salt to taste.

Simmer the kondai kadalai Kuzhambu for 10 to 15 minutes until the masala gets well incorporated into the kondai kadalai and the raw taste from the tamarind goes away.

Once done, turn off the heat, check the salt and spices and adjust the taste accordingly.

Serve the kondai kadalai Puli Vengaya Kuzhambu along with Beetroot Poriyal and hot steamed rice for lunch or dinner.

Cucumber Mor Kuzhambu Recipe (Cucumber Curry)

Cucumber Mor Kuzhambu is a delectable curry usually served with steamed rice. Cucumber pieces are cooked till soft and then mixed with a coconut-mustard-curd gravy. This simple curry is very flavourful and uses ingredients easily available in the pantry. This is a great way to use up leftover cucumbers lurking in the refrigerator. You can alternatively use white pumpkin.

Serve Cucumber Mor Kuzhambu with steamed rice and Keerai Sambar for a comforting weekday meal.

Prep Time   :   15 Mins

Cooks Time   :   20 Mins

Total Time   :   35 Mins

Cuisine   :   South Indian

Serving   :   4 Servings

Equipments Used: Saucepan With Handle (Tea/Sauces), KitchenAid Diamond Blender

Ingredients

3 to 4 Cucumber , peeled and chopped

1/2 cup Fresh coconut , scrapped

1 inch Ginger , chopped

1 teaspoon Mustard seeds (Rai/ Kadugu)

3 to 4 Green Chillies , chopped

1/4 teaspoon Turmeric powder (Haldi)

5 to 6 sprig Coriander (Dhania) Leaves

2 to 3 tablespoons Hung Curd (Greek Yogurt)

Salt , to taste

How to make Cucumber Mor Kuzhambu Recipe (Cucumber Curry)

To begin making the Cucumber Mor Kuzhambu recipe, firstly add the cucumber pieces along with 1/2 cup water and salt to a saucepan. Cook covered till the cucumber becomes just tender.

Grind together the coconut, ginger, chillies, mustard, coriander, turmeric in a blender to a fine paste. Add little water if required to make a fine paste.

Add this coconut paste to the cucumber. Cook on low heat for 2 to 3 minutes. Adjust water and salt if required.

Add the curd and mix.

Serve the Cucumber Mor Kuzhambu with steamed rice and Keerai Sambar for a comforting weekday meal.

Vepampoo Kara Kuzhambu Recipe (Dried Neem Flower Gravy)

Vepampoo has a myriad of benefits and is perfectly suitable for all age groups. I generally include vepampoo weekly once in any one of my dishes as it has antibacterial, anti-parasitic, anti-fungal, anti-inflammatory, and analgesic properties. One of the dishes which I make out neem flowers is Kara Kuzhambu. This dish does not show the bitterness of neem flower if cooked properly. The tangy taste of tamarind combined with roasted neem flowers is really drool worthy.

Serve Vepampoo Kara Kuzhambu along with hot steamed rice, Chow Chow Thoran and Elai Vadam for a perfect weekday meal.

Prep Time	:	20 Mins
Cooks Time	:	35 Mins
Total Time	:	55 Mins
Cuisine	:	South Indian
Serving	:	4 Servings

Equipments Used: Hard Anodised Kadai (Wok), Tadka Pan (Seasoning Pan)

Ingredients

12 to 15 Pearl onions (Sambar Onions)

4 to 5 cloves Garlic , finely chopped

1/4 teaspoon Turmeric powder (Haldi)

3/4 tablespoon Sambar Powder

1 teaspoon Coriander Powder (Dhania)

Tamarind , lemon sized

Water , as required

Salt , to taste

For tempering 1

3 teaspoons Sesame (Gingelly) Oil

1/4 teaspoon Asafoetida (hing)

1/3 teaspoon Mustard seeds (Rai/ Kadugu)

1/2 teaspoon Methi Seeds (Fenugreek Seeds)

1/4 teaspoon Chana dal (Bengal Gram Dal)

2 Dry Red Chillies

For tempering 2

1 teaspoon Sesame (Gingelly) Oil

1 tablespoon Neem leaves , dry

How to make Vepampoo Kara Kuzhambu Recipe (Dried Neem Flower Gravy)

To begin making the Vepampoo Kara Kuzhambu recipe, firstly make the tamarind juice with required water.

Heat oil in a heavy bottomed pan and add all the ingredients mentioned under 'For tempering 1' in the order given above.

After a minute, add the garlic and salute it for about a minute.

Next, add small onions and Sauté until it's fried nicely and becomes soft.

Add turmeric powder, sambar powder, coriander powder and salt. Mix everything well.

Add the tamarind juice, remaining water and curry leaves. Let it cook nicely until it becomes thick.

Take a small tadka pan and add oil & neem flowers and roast it. You can dry roast this also.

Switch off the Kuzhambu gas and add the neem flowers.

Your Vepampoo Kara Kuzhambu is ready to be served. Serve Vepampoo Kara Kuzhambu along with hot steamed rice, Chow Chow Thoran and Elai Vadam for a perfect weekday meal.

Kathirikai Urulai Kizhangu Kara Kuzhambu Recipe

Lunch is a traditional Chettinad dish which is commonly prepared in all households of Chettinad with brinjal and potatoes. Brinjals and potatoes are cubed and cooked with spices in a tamarind – tomato base. The addition of tamarind and tomato lends a sour taste to the gravy and addition of spices lends a spicy taste. The combination of sour and spicy makes it a perfect accompaniment for rice. The gravy lasts for a couple of days due to the addition of tamarind and sour.

Serve the Kathirikai Urulaikizhangu Kara kuzhambu with steamed rice, ghee and cabbage poriyal for a sunday lunch.

Prep Time	:	30 Mins
Cooks Time	:	40 Mins
Total Time	:	70 Mins
Cuisine	:	Chettinad
Serving	:	4 Servings

Equipments Used: Small Skillet (Shallow Fry Pan/ Omelette Pan)

Ingredients

6 Brinjal (Baingan / Eggplant) , cubed

1 Potato (Aloo) , cubed

15 Shallots , finely chopped

1 Tomato , finely chopped

1 teaspoon Sambar Powder

1 teaspoon Red Chilli powder

1/4 teaspoon Turmeric powder (Haldi)

1/2 teaspoon Salt

2 1/2 cup Water

Tamarind , lemon sized

To Temper

2 tablespoon Oil

1/8 teaspoon Asafoetida (hing)

Curry leaves , handful

3 Dry Red Chilli

1/4 teaspoon Methi Seeds (Fenugreek Seeds)

1 teaspoon Mustard seeds (Rai/ Kadugu)

1 teaspoon White Urad Dal (Split)

How to make Kathirikai Urulai Kizhangu Kara Kuzhambu Recipe

To begin the preparation of Kathirikai Urulai Kizhangu Kuzhambu, in a medium sized pan, heat oil over medium heat. Once the oil is hot, add mustard seeds.

Once the mustard seeds splutter, Add the remaining ingredients mentioned under tempering to the oil

Fry until the urad dal turns slightly brownish

Add chopped onions and cook until they are translucent

Add chopped tomatoes and cook until they become tender

Now, add cubed Brinjals and potato to the mixture in the pan

Add sambar powder, chili powder and salt to the mixture. Stir them well so that the vegetables are evenly coated with the spice blend.

Cook with the lid covered until brinjals and potato become tender.

Heat a ½ cup of water and add tamarind to the hot water. Extract tamarind juice and set aside

Add the extracted tamarind juice to the blend in the pan. Add 2 cups of water to the gravy

Cook the curry over low heat until Brinjals and Potatoes are cooked well.

Simmer the curry till the oil separates from the gravy.

Serve the Kathirikai Urulai Kizhangu Kuzhambhu with hot rice and fried papad

Chettinad Thakkali Vengaya Kuzhambu Recipe

The Chettinad Thakkali Vengaya Kuzhambu Recipe is a tandy curry that is made from simmering baby onions also known as the sambar onion or Chinna Vengayam in tamil. Great to be served with steamed rice and poriyal.

The Chettinad Thakkali Vengaya Kuzhambu Recipe is a tandy curry that is made from simmering baby onions also known as the sambar onion or Chinna Vengayam in tamil. Chettinad cuisine is one of the most popular cuisines of Southern India, that is packed with a few essential ingredients and that is the baby onion and the black peppercorns.

The Chettinad Thakkali Vengaya Kuzhambu is a perfect dish to go along with some steaming hot rice, Cabbage Poriyal and Appalam. Serve it for lunch or dinner and you will surely enjoy this spicy curry.

Prep Time   :   10 Mins

Cooks Time   :   30 Mins

Total Time   :   40 Mins

Cuisine   :   Chettinad

Serving : 4 Servings

Equipments Used: Hard Anodized Pressure
Cooker, Small Skillet (Shallow Fry Pan/ Omelette
Pan)

Ingredients

2 cups Tamarind Water

12 Pearl onions (Sambar Onions) , peeled and
halved

2 Tomatoes , roughly chopped

1 teaspoon Sambar Powder

1 teaspoon Whole Black Peppercorns , coarsely
pounded

Salt , to taste

1 teaspoon Jaggery

Ingredients for seasoning

1 teaspoon Sesame (Gingelly) Oil

1 teaspoon Mustard seeds (Rai/ Kadugu)

1/2 teaspoon Methi Seeds (Fenugreek Seeds)

2 sprig Curry leaves , roughly torn

How to make Chettinad Thakkali Vengaya Kuzhambu Recipe

To begin making the Chettinad Thakkali Vengaya Kuzhambu Recipe, first get all the ingredients prepped and ready. Make the tamarind water according to the recipe - How To Make Tamarind Water

Once the ingredients are prepped, we will cook them all in the pressure cooker. Into the pressure cooker, add the tomatoes, onions, tamarind water, salt, jaggery, sambar powder, pepper and salt. Stir well to combine and cook until you hear a couple of whistles.

After a couple of whistles, turn off the heat and allow the pressure to release naturally. Once released, stir well and transfer to a boil. The Kuzhambu will be a little runny, if you like a thicker Chettinad Vengaya Kuzhambu, then you can simmer the Kuzhambu on low heat until it thickens.

Check the salt and spices and adjust to suit your taste.

The final step is the seasoning. Heat a little oil in a small tadka pan, add the mustard seeds, fenugreek seeds and allow it to crackle. Once it crackles add the curry leaves and stir.

Turn off the heat and add the seasoning to the Chettinad Vengaya Kuzhambu and serve.

Serve the Chettinad Thakkali Vengaya Kuzhambu along with some steaming hot rice, Cabbage Poriyal and Appalam. Serve it for lunch or dinner and you will surely enjoy this spicy curry.

Printed in Great Britain
by Amazon